# after
# adoption

### the needs of adopted youth

**Jeanne A. Howard**
**Susan Livingston Smith**

**CWLA Press**
**Washington, DC**

CWLA Press is an imprint of the Child Welfare League of America. The Child Welfare League of America is the nation's oldest and largest membership-based child welfare organization. We are committed to engaging people everywhere in promoting the well-being of children, youth, and their families, and protecting every child from harm.

CHILD WELFARE LEAGUE OF AMERICA, INC.
HEADQUARTERS
440 First Street NW, Third Floor
Washington, DC 20001-2085
E-mail: books@cwla.org

CURRENT PRINTING (last digit)

10 9 8 7 6 5 4 3 2 1

Printed in the United States of America

Cover and text design by James D. Melvin

ISBN# 0-87868-883-8

Library of Congress Cataloging-in-Publication Data

Howard, Jeanne A.
After adoption : the needs of adopted youth / Jeanne A. Howard and
Susan Livingston Smith.
    p. cm.
Includes bibliographical references.
ISBN 0-87868-883-8 (alk. paper)
1. Adopted children--United States--Family relationships. I. Smith,
Susan Livingston. II. Title.
HV875.55.H684 2003
362.73'4--dc21

2003011229

# CONTENTS

# TABLES

# FIGURES

# ACKNOWLEDGMENTS

*After Adoption: The Needs of Adopted Youth* is the culmination of the efforts of many people. It was undertaken by researchers at the Illinois State University Center for Adoption Studies, which is funded by the Illinois Department of Children and Family Services (DCFS). It has been our great good fortune to be associated with DCFS during its incredible shift in moving waiting children into adoptive homes. We are particularly grateful to former Director Jess McDonald, both for his support of our work and his dedication to the children of our state. His commitment to adoptive families has moved Illinois to a position of leadership in the provision of postadoption services.

This study was one of the first major undertakings of the staff of the Center for Adoption Studies and involved the hard work of all our staff. In particular, we thank Ivy Hutchison for her dedication in carrying out the "nuts and bolts" of organizing this effort, and Karla Uphoff, whose oversight of data collection and whose skill in data analysis were invaluable. We also thank Judy Pence for coordinating the effort to obtain the sample of families. The energy and goodwill of all the center staff helped immensely.

Above all, we thank the parents who took the time to complete this lengthy and detailed survey. We were struck by the candor of their remarks in describing the challenges they face and were greatly encouraged both by their commitment to their children and their positive reports of how their children fared after adoption. It is our hope that the information they share here will help everyone who works to promote adoption do a better job of preparing and supporting families.

# INTRODUCTION

How do children adopted from the child welfare system fare after adoption? That is the central question this research seeks to answer. The push for adoption embodied by the Adoption and Safe Families Act of 1997 and the large increase in the number of adoptions occurring since its passage indicate that children in the foster care system can be moved into adoptive homes. But the legal act of adoption is not the end of the story. Conscientious social policy development requires that we learn not only how to accomplish social policy goals but also how to assess their effects over time. In terms of achieving permanence through adoption, we have an obligation not only to move children to adoption, but also to determine how they adjust and function once this has been achieved.

Adoptive parents have much to teach us. Data gathered from adoptive families can provide us with information to better prepare families for adoption and to design supports that can sustain families for the long haul. The more than 1,300 adoptive parents who took the time to complete this lengthy survey gave us much to think about. The good news is that on average, parents reported their children were doing well after adoption—managing satisfactorily not only in their adoptive homes, but also in their schools and communities. Children were generally healthy, both physically and mentally. Perhaps even more important, families were committed to their children, even when problems were present. Most parents reported feeling close to their children and believed that adoption had a positive effect on their family. The significant majority of parents reported that, even knowing everything they now know, they would adopt their child again.

Life with a child adopted from the child welfare system is not without struggle, however. Many children experienced multiple types of maltreatment before their adoptions and had a series of damaging experiences in their early lives. Prenatal substance exposure, early deprivation, abuse, neglect, and chaotic family circumstances were aspects of the histories of many children. Such early life experiences sometimes complicated children's ability to learn, to accept nurturance, to get along with others, or to take responsibility for their actions. But although some children struggled and demonstrated serious behavioral and emotional problems, most children did not.

Adoptive families come in many forms. When the researchers examined the data by type of adoptive family (comparing children adopted by kin, children adopted by foster parents, and children adopted by parents matched with them for the purpose of adoption), they found several interesting differences. Most notably, kin adopters reported more positively on their children's functioning than foster parents or matched parents in almost every category.

## Study Highlights

- Respondents were 1,343 parents of children adopted from the public child welfare system, who were receiving adoption subsidies and whose children were 6 years old or older.
- Substantial numbers of families had low incomes, indicating the importance of adoption subsidies. Slightly more than 40% of families reported annual incomes (excluding subsidies) less than $25,000, and 54% had incomes less than $35,000. Kin adopters had significantly lower incomes than foster or matched parents, with 62% reporting incomes of less than $25,000 annually.
- Most children were adopted into families of the same race or ethnicity. The majority of those who were placed across race or ethnicity were African American. Children placed across race generally fared well, but they had higher scores on an index of behavior problems than children placed with same-race families did.
- Most children were young when first removed from their birthfamilies— 50% were first removed before age 1, and 76% before age 5. Children were also young when first placed in what became their adoptive families, with 27% placed before age 1, and 66% before age 5.

- The average time from first removal to adoption finalization was 4.5 years.
- Serious neglect was the most commonly reported type of maltreatment experienced by children (63% of cases), followed by prenatal exposure to drugs and alcohol (60%).
- Parents rated children on their functioning in the home, school, and community, as well as their health and mental health. Parents rated the significant majority of children as doing well or very well in all domains.
- Parents reported most problems in school. In 54% of cases, children's behaviors interfered with their learning; 40% of children were in special education classes, and 25% had been suspended.
- Although most children were rated as doing well in the community, 20% of teens had experienced involvement with the police or legal system.
- Most children (92%) were rated as having good or excellent health. Most families relied on Medicaid to pay for medical expenses, and many parents reported problems finding providers that accepted Medicaid.
- Although most parents rated their child as mentally healthy, 25% identified their child's mental health as fair or poor.
- Of children, 53% had seen a counselor for emotional or behavioral problems, and 12% experienced psychiatric hospitalization or residential treatment.
- Children had elevated scores on the Behavior Problem Index (BPI), averaging 11.91, compared with a national mean score of 6.44. Children adopted by kin had lower BPI scores than those adopted by foster or matched parents.
- The most powerful risk factor in predicting a high BPI score was prenatal substance exposure. The child's ability to give and receive affection was the most powerful protective factor influencing the level of behavior problems.
- African American children had fewer reported problems than Caucasian children. For example, African American children were less likely to be rated as "difficult to raise," and they had lower mean BPI scores. This was particularly true for African American children adopted by kin.

- Parents were very positive in their assessment of the adoption experience. Of parents, 91% reported they were very satisfied or satisfied with the adoption, and 93% would definitely or probably adopt again knowing what they now know. Of respondents, 72% reported that adopting the child affected their family positively, and 82% reported feeling very close to their child.

- A small minority of parents (12%) rated their children as "very difficult to raise." Although these children had serious and often long-standing problems, half were rated as having a good or excellent adjustment at home.

The next chapters examine these findings in detail, then conclude with a review of parent concerns and recommendations for improving services to families and children both before and after adoption.

# PART I
# STUDY OVERVIEW

# CHAPTER ONE

# THE STUDY CONTEXT

The practice of adoption in the United States has changed dramatically over the past three decades. Societal changes, including advances in the use of birth control, the legalization of abortion, and a greater acceptance of single parenting, have resulted in a declining number of infants available for adoption.

At the same time, growing numbers of maltreated children were removed from their birthfamilies. In the late 1970s, the large number of children drifting in foster care became a concern of child welfare experts. Several important studies highlighted the high cost of such care and the negative effect of impermanence on children in the system (Bush & Gordon, 1982; Fanshel & Shinn, 1978; Maluccio, Fein, Hamilton, Klier, & Ward, 1980; Vasaly, 1978). Fanshel and Shinn (1978) and others provided evidence that the longer a child stayed in foster care, the greater the likelihood that the child would remain in the system, as well as lose contact with birthfamily members.

## Recent Developments in Adoption

Growing concerns about the plight of children in the child welfare system led to national child welfare policies to reduce impermanence. These policies, which were codified in the federal Adoption Assistance and Child Welfare Act of 1980 (P.L. 96-272), advanced the permanency planning movement. In addition to the emphases on family preservation and timely reunification of removed children with their birthfamilies whenever possible, the movement led to the termination of parental rights for a growing number of abused and neglected children and placement of many of these children in adoptive

1

homes. The government made financial subsidies available to families adopting children with special needs, to enable these children to find permanent homes.

Children who, in previous years, would have been consigned to the uncertainties of growing up in foster care were now being placed for adoption. Many of these children were special needs children, a designation that qualifies the child for an adoption subsidy. Although the definition of *special needs* varies from state to state, it generally denotes conditions that make children harder to place—older age; minority or sibling group status; or medical, mental, or emotional problems. In many ways, this term is an arbitrary distinction, because states vary widely in their qualifications to receive subsidies. For example, age limits vary from birth for minority children in some states to age 12 for white children in a few states (Avery, 1998).

Due to policy and practice changes, adoption of children who were wards of the state has increased over the past two decades. Parents adopted approximately 20,000 children with special needs each year throughout the mid-1990s (Child Welfare League of America, 1997). This number comprised approximately one-third of unrelated adoptions in the United States at that time. (National adoption statistics indicate that about half of the approximately 114,000 adoptions each year are by relatives, and the other half are by nonrelated people [Flango & Flango, 1995].)

Despite the gains resulting from the permanency planning movement, by the mid-1990s, record numbers of children were in foster care. Renewed concern about the effect of impermanence on children and the resulting costs of foster care led to passage of the Adoption and Safe Families Act (ASFA). ASFA imposed time limits for parental improvements and created incentives for states to move children to adoption. Following the passage of ASFA in 1997, the number of children moving from foster care to adoption increased dramatically. The Adoption and Foster Care Analysis and Reporting System of the U.S. Children's Bureau (2002) reported that in fiscal year 2000, parents adopted approximately 51,000 children in the foster care system. In the tradition of the large child welfare state of Illinois, more children moved to adoption and subsidized guardianship in fiscal year (FY) 1999 than in the 10 years between FYs 1986 and 1995 combined.

# Current Research Knowledge

The adoption of children with special needs has become a national priority, resulting in dramatic increases in the movement of children from foster care to adoption. But how do children and their families fare? Researchers have limited knowledge about the adjustment outcomes of children adopted through public child welfare systems and the needs of the families who adopt them. A number of outcome studies on adoption mainly look at children adopted domestically as infants or adopted internationally. The body of research on children adopted through the child welfare system and their families has focused primarily on the factors related to adoption disruption. A few states have conducted small needs assessment surveys of families on adoption assistance, but these have not found their way into published professional sources.

Only a handful of studies in the child welfare literature have examined postadoption outcomes and needs in families who adopted through public child welfare departments. Nelson (1985) conducted the first of these in the early 1980s. She examined 257 children in 177 adoptive families recruited from Detroit, Chicago, and Houston, between one and four years after finalization. The children met one of the following special needs criteria: sibling group of three or more, a child eight or older at the time of placement, or a child with an impairment. Nelson found that 62% of the children were reported to have moderate to severe behavior problems. Despite these problems, a large majority of parents evaluated their adoptions as satisfying.

Nelson (1985), however, reported 27% of the adoptions as having a pronounced negative aspect (giving less than a "good" response on items in an adoption satisfaction scale), which she perceived as placing the adoptions at risk of dissolution. Of the adoptions, 3% had already ended. In analyzing seven dissolutions occurring in these families, Nelson reported that the child welfare system inadequately prepared parents in almost all these situations, and most parents did not receive adequate information about their children.

Nelson (1985) analyzed the factors associated with parental satisfaction. The only family characteristic predicting satisfaction was more frequent church attendance. Child characteristics included: not being isolated (having friends, not keeping people at arm's length, etc.), being a girl (parents of girls were more satisfied than parents of boys), not having a previous disruption, and not being a legal risk placement. The main agency-related predictors of satisfaction were preplacement factors—being adequately prepared and getting adequate information about the child. In relation to postadoption services, belonging to a parent group was related to increased parental satisfaction, and having to do without needed services was related to dissatisfaction. Of all the above factors, the child's isolation was the strongest predictor of parental dissatisfaction.

Rosenthal and Groze (1991, 1992, 1994) conducted a longitudinal outcome study of families adopting through the child welfare system. They evaluated 757 adoptive families who adopted through child welfare departments in Illinois, Oklahoma, and Kansas. Not all families received subsidies, and each state had different special needs criteria. Respondents completed the Achenbach Child Behavior Checklist (CBC) as well as an extensive questionnaire. Overall, 41% of children scored in the "clinical range" on the total problems score of the CBC, placing them in the top 10% of scores in a normal child population. Despite the children's behavior problems, only 4% of parents reported that the adoption had a negative effect on their family.

A follow-up study completed three to four years later reported some increase in child behavior problems and a decrease in parental satisfaction. Rosenthal and Groze (1994) concluded that behavioral problems for many special needs adoptees do not subside over time in their adoptive families.

Another longitudinal study conducted by Groze (1996) analyzed a group of subsidized adoptive families in Iowa each year for four years, with a final analysis of 71 families who participated all four years. His study had similar findings to those described above, showing a persistence of behavioral problems and some decline in family adaptability and cohesion. For example, in year one, only 3% of families evaluated the overall effect of the adoption on the family as negative; however, in year four, 14% of families did so. Still, the vast majority of families were satisfied with their adoptions. Groze also explored families' perceptions of gaps in needed services. The most needed services (identified by 20%–35%) in order of frequency were additional financial supports, counseling related to adoption, dental and medical care, child support groups, counseling about parenting skills, parent support groups, and special education.

In summary, the only postadoption outcome study of families adopting solely through public child welfare departments that had a large, randomly selected sample is the study conducted by Rosenthal and Groze (1991, 1994).

The initial data collection for this study was in 1988. The limited literature on child welfare adoptions does indicate that a substantial number of children continue to have significant behavior problems, but that the vast majority of adoptive parents are satisfied with their adoptions.

The study described in this book seeks to increase the knowledge of the needs of families adopting through child welfare auspices. It focuses on families adopting children through the Illinois Department of Children and Family Services who are receiving adoption assistance. Illinois is a large child welfare state, having the third-largest number of children in foster care at the time of data collection. This study seeks to explore children's well-being and level of adjustment in key areas of their lives (home, school, neighborhood and community, health and mental health), as well as to determine what services their families need to enhance their children's adjustment. It has the largest sample of any study of children adopted through public child welfare auspices.

## Study Design

### Survey Development

The researchers developed the survey for this study to learn more about children's adjustment after adoption. Previous research involving adoptive families who were struggling indicated that children demonstrate strength as well as difficulty across many aspects of their lives. This survey assessed children's adjustment and functioning at school, at home, and in the community. The researchers included a set of questions about family preparation for adoption. They wrote a draft of the survey based on current knowledge about family needs after adoption. The researchers consulted with Richard Barth, who was one of the authors of a longitudinal study of adoption in California. After this consultation, they added questions from the California study, in particular, the Behavior Problem Index.

In addition to the 65 forced choice and Likert-type scale questions, they survey included two open-ended questions. They provided parents with the opportunity to provide context and detail. The questions are:

- What is the best thing about your child? Because so many of the survey questions could highlight difficulties or challenges, the authors felt it was important to capture the positive attributes and abilities of children that might not otherwise be captured.

• What other recommendations, if any, do you have for improving services to adopted children and their families?

In addition to these general questions, several other questions included open-ended responses. For example, if parents identified educational needs of their children that were not adequately met, they survey asked them to describe services they felt would benefit their children.

Twelve volunteer families who had adopted children with special needs piloted the first draft. Parents either completed the survey, marking areas they felt needed more clarification or emphasis, or went through the survey making margin notes and suggestions. The authors modified sections of the instrument in response to their comments.

After the second draft, the researchers evaluated the revised survey for reading level. Using the Flesch-Kincaid assessment of reading level, they found the survey understandable by those at a grade level of 4.8.

## Sampling Procedure

Because some of the difficulties faced by children with problematic early lives do not manifest until the child enters school, the researchers limited the study to children ages 6 and older. Because of the length of the survey, the researchers asked parents to complete the form on only one adopted child in their family. Because previous studies suggest that problems increase with age, the study asked parents to complete the survey on their oldest adopted child for whom they receive a subsidy.

In December 1999, the Illinois Department of Children and Family Services (DCFS) identified 19,739 children ages 6 and older receiving adoption assistance in 11,354 homes. The department systematically selected a sample of 3,993 families from this group. Department employees mailed surveys with a letter from the DCFS director explaining the study and encouraging participation and a postage-paid return envelope to each family. The department mailed the surveys, rather than the researchers, to protect the confidentiality of families receiving adoption assistance. The initial mailing yielded a return of 860. The department sent a follow-up postcard to every family in the sample, thanking those who had completed the survey and urging those who had not yet returned one to do so. It provided a phone number for those who had misplaced their surveys to call to receive another. The post office returned some surveys as undeliverable. Overall, respondents returned 1,343 surveys (34% of delivered surveys). The researchers did not use three surveys completed for young adults in their mid-20s, so this report is based on 1,340 usable responses.

## Comparison of Respondents to Population

There were only a few statistics that researchers could compute using the database on the population from which the sample was drawn. Some variables, such as race of parent, had missing data in a substantial number of cases in the database. Table 1.1 reports the characteristics for which a comparison could be made between the respondents and the population of subsidized adoptions of children ages 6 and older as of December 1999.

Table 1.1 indicates that the age of children studied is representative of the total population; however, African American children are somewhat under-represented among the respondents. A significant number of respondents (10%) did not report race of their adopted child. The actual percentage of African American children is likely to be higher than the 52% reported, but not as high as the 69% reported for the total population. The proportion of Hispanic children among the respondents is very similar to that of the general population of adopted children.

In addition, it is possible to make a general comparison of the proportion of relative adoptions of study families based on the median year of finalization (1995) and the proportion of relative adoptions occurring in that year. The percentage of relative adoptive families responding to this survey (39%) is similar to the 41.5% of adoptions by kin in the population of families adopting that year. The proportion of kin adoptions has gradually increased throughout the past decade. This percentage peaked among adoptions finalized in 1999, however, most adoptions in this study were finalized in 1995 or earlier.

## Description of Responding Families

Of responding families, 13.6% now reside outside Illinois. The researchers received surveys from families in 77 of Illinois's 102 counties, and counties that are not represented have small populations. Based on 1990 census data, 97% of the state population is composed of residents in the counties represented in this study. Of the respondents, 47% reside in Cook County (Chicago area), which contains 45% of the state's overall population.

Of responding families, 83% were formed through adoption of a foster child (44%) or relative (39%). Matched adoptions with recruited adoptive

**Table 1.1**
Comparisons of Respondents to Population

| Characteristic | Population | Respondents |
|---|---|---|
| Age of oldest adoptee on subsidy | 12.0 | 12.1 |
| Race of oldest adoptee on subsidy (in percentages) | | |
| African American | 69.0 | 51.7 |
| White | 24.6 | 30.7 |
| Hispanic | 5.4 | 5.3 |
| Other | 0.8 | 2.5 |
| Unknown | 0.2 | 9.8 |

families were the least common, representing only 14%. A few respondents described their child as joining their family in ways not classified under the previous categories (3%). Many of these had been an acquaintance of the child prior to their decision to adopt the child, such as the child being the foster child of the adoptive parent's relative or neighbor.

The survey was most often completed by mothers (90%). The most common age category of adoptive parents completing the form was 40 to 49 years, representing 38% of the sample. Two-thirds of responding parents were between ages 40 and 59. Of parents, 18% were older than age 60. Specific breakdowns by age are given in Table 1.2.

The majority of households (59%) were headed by two parents, with the rest headed by single parents. Of families overall, 10% had other adults (not spouses or partners) living in the home, nearly all of whom were adult family members. Single parents were more likely to have other adult family members not identified as spouses or partners living in the home, which was the case for 15% of these families. The majority of families had more than one adopted child (58%), and 42% had birthchildren as well as adopted children. Foster children were present in 21% of the families. Of families, 12.5% contained other children, typically grandchildren or other relatives.

A substantial number of families had relatively low incomes. The survey asked parents to report their yearly income, excluding adoption assistance. For 41% of families, family income was less than $25,000, and in 56%, it was less

**Table 1.2**
Age of Adoptive Parent

| Age | n | Percentage |
|---|---|---|
| Younger than 30 | 14 | 1 |
| 30–39 | 190 | 15 |
| 40–49 | 495 | 38 |
| 50–59 | 367 | 28 |
| 60–69 | 175 | 13 |
| 70–79 | 52 | 4 |
| 80 or older | 2 | <1% |

than $35,000. This can be compared with the general population of the state, in which 28.5% of families have incomes less than $25,000, and 44% of families have incomes less than $35,000. The mean household size in the state of Illinois is 2.6 people. Given that the mean family size for respondents in this study was more than five people, reported income figures suggest that adoption assistance is an important source of support for many families raising adopted children.

The significant majority of parents (70%) had training or education beyond high school. Of the respondents, 15% had completed college, and another 15% had education beyond a four-year degree; however, 15% of parents did not complete high school.

Most parents (90%) were of the same race or ethnicity as their child. In 6% of families, African American children were placed transracially, followed by 3% of Hispanic children. (Children were classified as transracially placed when they were a different race from either of their adoptive parents.) White, Native American, and Asian American children were placed across race/ethnicity in less than 1% of families each. Because the survey allowed parents to identify themselves or their children by as many races or ethnicities as necessary, the researchers did not classify children with more than one race or ethnicity as to whether they were transracially placed.

## Description of Children

The children were fairly evenly divided by sex, with 50.7% male and 49.3% female. The parents did not report race for 10% of the children. For those reporting race, 57% of children were African American, followed by 34% white and 6% Hispanic. Parents reported 3% of children as being of other races. Native American and Asian children were each less than 1% of the respondent group. The mean age of children at the time of survey completion was 12.1 years.

Generally speaking, the child welfare system removed children in the survey at young ages, placed them in what became their adoptive homes at young ages, but did not make them permanent legal members of their families until they were much older. The age at removal from their birthfamilies was early for the vast majority of children. Workers removed 50.3% between birth and age 1, with 32% removed prior to 6 months of age. Workers had removed 76% prior to age 5.

Children also were relatively young when first placed in their current adoptive homes. The system placed 27% in their current home when they were younger than age 1, 38% when they were younger than 2, and 66% when they were younger than 5. The age at finalized adoption, however, was much older. Only 13% of children achieved finalization at age 2 or younger. At age 6, 51% had achieved finalization, and at age nine, 78%.

The average time period from children's first removal from their birthfamily to finalization was 4.5 years. It is important to note that the original plan for the child may not have been adoption. Survey data do not capture the period from developing an adoption plan to finalization. Overall, the mean length of time since adoption finalization for these children was 5.4 years, and children had resided in their adoptive families for a mean of 8.6 years. Of responding families, 45% adopted sibling groups.

Parents reported children's adverse experiences (maltreatment, repeated moves in care, etc.) occurring before this placement that presented challenges to adjustment. As indicated in Table 1.3, for many items, a sizeable number of parents reported that they did not know if their child had had this experience. For example, one in four parents reported they did were unsure if their child had been sexually abused.

**Table 1.3**
Adverse Conditions Prior to Adoptive Placement (in percentages)

| Condition | Yes | No | Unsure |
|---|---|---|---|
| Serious neglect | 63 | 29 | 8 |
| Exposed to drugs or alcohol before birth | 60 | 19 | 21 |
| Two or more foster homes | 37 | 60 | 4 |
| Physical abuse | 33 | 51 | 16 |
| Back and forth between birthhome and foster care | 18 | 76 | 6 |
| Sexual abuse | 17 | 59 | 25 |
| Previous adoptive placement | 14 | 82 | 4 |
| Psychiatric treatment center placement | 9 | 87 | 4 |

Of parents, 14% reported that their child had experienced an adoption disruption. Because no accurate information on the adoption disruption rate in Illinois is currently available, the researchers were interested in the accuracy of this figure. The question asks, "BEFORE your child first came to your home, was he/she placed in another adoptive home?" The researchers believed that most parents understood the question, because its frequency was highest among those whose children were having difficulty.

As evidenced in Table 1.3, serious neglect and prenatal substance exposure were the most common negative influences experienced by these children. Parents reported that 90% of children had at least one adverse condition or experience, and 60% had two or more. Nearly 4 in 10 children (39%) had three or more such factors.

In addition to adverse experiences, the survey asked parents whether their children had particular disabilities and asked them to rate the disabilities' severities when present. These are reported in Table 1.4.

The most common item was behavior problems, rated as present in more than half of children. These problems are analyzed later in relation to children's scores on the Behavior Problem Index.

**Table 1.4**
Special Conditions of Children (in percentages)

| Condition | Percentage of Total | Degree When Present | | |
|---|---|---|---|---|
| | | Mild | Moderate | Severe |
| Behavior problems | 51 | 43 | 38 | 19 |
| Learning disabilities | 47 | 35 | 46 | 19 |
| Emotional disturbances | 35 | 40 | 39 | 21 |
| Developmental delays | 32 | 40 | 43 | 17 |
| Vision/hearing impairments | 32 | 49 | 37 | 14 |
| Chronic medical problems | 18 | 30 | 45 | 24 |
| Physical handicaps | 7 | 45 | 27 | 28 |
| Mental retardation | 8 | 40 | 41 | 19 |

## Families' Preparation for Adoption

To assess families' perceptions of their preparation for adoption, the survey asked parents to evaluate the preparation that they and their children received prior to adoption. Overall, parents felt they had been given important information about their children's past (67%), received written information about the child's history (55%), had been given ideas about where to get help (60%), and were visited regularly after adoptive placement and prior to finalization (78%). Parents reported that workers discussed possible future difficulties (56%) and gave them ideas for how to get help for their children (60%). Workers explained to children what it meant to be adopted in 52% of cases. Other aspects of preparation took place in less than half the cases. In those cases where it was applicable, parents reported workers were less likely to arrange for them to meet with the child's previous caregivers (40%) or to gradually allow the child to get to know the family (47%). Children were helped with grief, separation, and loss issues in 38% of cases. Lifebooks or other such tools to explore the child's past were reported in only 25% of cases.

In addition, 49% of parents reported receiving training prior to adoption. Of those, considerable variation existed in the number of hours of training reported, ranging from 1 hour to 300 (see Table 1.5).

**Table 1.5**
Hours of Training Received (in percentages)

| | |
|---|---|
| 1–5 | 12 |
| 6–10 | 38 |
| 11–20 | 30 |
| More than 21 | 20 |

When parents did receive training, 52% found it very helpful, and 44% somewhat helpful. The survey asked parents what other information needed to be included in training. Only 10% responded. The most common suggestions were that training be longer or more extensive, that training include more information related to specific conditions such as fetal alcohol syndrome or attachment disorder, and that training be located or arranged to better meet parents' schedules.

Overall, most parents felt fully or somewhat prepared by professionals for adoption (59% and 32%, respectively). Only 9% reported that they were poorly prepared. Parents were even more positive about their children's preparation. Children were rated as fully prepared for adoption in 63% of cases, and somewhat prepared in 29%, with 8% rated as poorly prepared.

Of parents, however, 30% commented that additional things could have been done to better prepare the family for adoption. The most frequent suggestion was the need for full disclosure of the child's past and full explanation about what that history might mean for the child later in his or her development. One parent in a matched adoptive family wrote, "We had no idea what the effects of the birthmother's drug and alcohol abuse would have on our child. [We needed to know] what services we might need in the future and where to seek them." In a related vein, several parents wrote about the need for specific preparation for promoting attachment and helping children resolve past losses. Parent comments that typified these concerns are:

> [Our preparation should have included] how very long the healing process for the child can be and the need for consistency.

**Table 1.6**
Services Included in Subsidy Agreements (in percentages)

| | |
|---|---|
| Counseling | 37 |
| Medical care not covered by Medicaid | 32 |
| Tutoring | 7 |
| Physical/occupational therapy | 7 |
| Specialized camp | 4 |
| Therapeutic day care | 4 |
| Other | 6 |

[We needed] training and preparation on bonding—building a relationship with [the child], resolution of loss.

We should have been told what he would feel at the loss of his [birth] family.

Other parent comments reflected the need to be prepared for later behavioral or developmental problems, the need for more follow-up after the permanency plan becomes adoption, and the need for better preparation about complex medical needs.

One parent expressed deep concerns about being pressured to adopt:

[I recommend] truth, full disclosure and no coercion. We were told, "I'll have to look for another family if you don't adopt BOTH children at the same time." This after the older child had been with us for three years!

A few other parents mentioned problems with inexperienced workers or workers who did not give them much preparation. As one parent put it, "My caseworker was new and poorly trained. I was the one who prepared my child for adoption."

Despite these suggestions, most parents were comfortable with the preparation they and their children received, and many of the basics of preparation were attended to in most families. Some important elements may be missing, however. Although those that attended adoption training rated it highly, less than half of families reported receiving such training. Although most were told

**Table 1.7**
Additional Subsidy Needs Identified by Families

| Type | n | Percentage of Requests |
|---|---|---|
| Tutoring | 129 | 29 |
| Counseling/specialized therapy | 101 | 23 |
| Medical assistance | 84 | 19 |
| Camp/summer program | 55 | 13 |
| Educational needs | 40 | 9 |
| Child care | 35 | 8 |
| Basic needs[a] | 24 | 5 |
| Respite | 18 | 4 |
| Residential care | 10 | 2 |
| Recreational activities | 10 | 2 |
| Transportation | 9 | 2 |
| College help/continue subsidy | 9 | 2 |
| Transition to independence | 8 | 2 |

[a] Includes assistance for food, clothing, furniture, modifications to house for wheelchair ramps, school fees, and housing.

important things about the child's past and received such information in writing, one parent in three reported not being told important information, and nearly half received no written information about the child's past. Of respondents, 44% stated that workers did not apprise them of possible future difficulties based on their child's past, and 40% did not receive ideas about where to get help after adoption.

## Adoption Subsidy

All families in the study received subsidy for their children. In addition to monetary support for basic maintenance, the subsidy agreement for 60% of families offered assistance with one or more other services, as listed in Table 1.6.

Some families (19%) had sought additions to their subsidy agreement since their adoption, and of these only 24% received additions. The additional services approved included tutoring/other educational services, counseling, medical care or equipment, camp, and occupational/physical or speech therapy, each occurring in less than 19% of cases. An increase in subsidy amount, therapeutic day care, and residential care were granted in two cases each.

Of families, 37% reported that they need additional assistance through subsidies. Their responses ($n$ = 438) to an open-ended question about needs appear in Table 1.7. Respondents identified as many as three needs, totaling 508 separate requests.

## References

Avery, R. J. (1998). Adoption assistance under P.L. 96-272: A policy analysis. *Children and Youth Services Review, 20,* 29–55.

Bush, M., & Gordon, A. C. (1982). The case for involving children in child welfare decisions. *Social Work, 27,* 309–314.

Child Welfare League of America. (1997). *Report on adoption statistics.* Available from http://www.cwla.org/programs/adoption/adoptionfactsheet.htm.

Fanshel, D., & Shinn, E. (1978). *Children in foster care: A longitudinal investigation.* New York: Columbia University Press.

Flango, V., & Flango, C. R. (1995). How many children were adopted in 1992? *Child Welfare, 77,* 1018–1032.

Groze, V. (1996). *Successful adoptive families: A longitudinal study of special needs adoption.* Westport, CT: Praeger.

Maluccio, A., Fein, E., Hamilton, J., Klier, J. L., & Ward, D. (1980). Beyond permanency planning. *Child Welfare, 59,* 515–530.

Nelson, K. A. (1985). *On the frontier of adoption: A study of special needs adoptive families.* New York: Child Welfare League of America.

Rosenthal, J. A., & Groze, V. K. (1991). Behavioral problems of special needs adopted children. *Children & Youth Services Review, 13,* 343–361.

Rosenthal, J. A., & Groze, V. K. (1992). *Special-needs adoption: A study of intact families.* Westport, CT: Praeger.

Rosenthal, J. A., & Groze, V. K. (1994). A longitudinal study of special-needs adoptive families. *Child Welfare, 73,* 689–706.

U.S. Children's Bureau. (2002). *AFCARS report #7: Interim 2000 estimates as of August 2002.* Washington, DC: Author.

Vasaly, S. (1978). *Foster care in five states: A synthesis and analysis of studies from Arizona, California, Iowa, Massachusetts and Vermont.* Washington, DC: U.S. Department of Health, Education and Welfare.

# CHAPTER TWO

# Children's Adjustments in Life Domains

Children's adjustments after adoption need to be examined in several dimensions. Respondents answered survey questions about their child's functioning in the home, school, and community and also rated their children's physical and mental health. Parents also indicated if their children's needs were being met in each area, and if not, what services or supports might be of help.

## Child's Adjustment at Home

Overall, children were doing well in their homes and families. Of parents, 89% rated their child's adjustment at home as excellent (56%) or good (33%). Parents rated children with less positive adjustments at home as fair (9%) or poor (2%). Only 11% of parents rated their children's adjustment at home as fair or poor, however, the majority indicated that they had concerns related to their children's adjustments at home.

Also, the survey asked parents to evaluate how well their child was able to function in several areas, compared with other children the same age. The children's abilities that were a concern most often were handling anger and frustration, making good decisions, and following instructions. The parents' ratings on these abilities are reported in Table 2.1.

The survey asked parents about how difficult it was to find a babysitter due to their child's needs. Of respondents, 19% reported that it was very difficult, 24% responded that it was somewhat difficult, and 57% said it was not difficult at all. Those parents reporting difficulty were more likely to have children with the following special needs: behavior problems (particularly severe

**Table 2.1**
Child's Abilities Compared with Others of Same Age (in percentages)

| Ability | Very Well | Fairly Well | Poorly | Not at All |
|---|---|---|---|---|
| Care for self | 58 | 34 | 7 | 1 |
| Give and receive affection | 57 | 31 | 10 | 1 |
| Get along with children | 45 | 42 | 12 | 1 |
| Keep self safe | 40 | 43 | 14 | 4 |
| Follow instructions | 33 | 45 | 22 | 1 |
| Make good decisions | 24 | 46 | 25 | 4 |
| Handle anger/frustration | 21 | 42 | 32 | 6 |

Note. Percentages may not equal 100 due to rounding.

behaviors), emotional disturbances, chronic medical problems, and physical handicaps. Although 19% said that their child's special needs made it very difficult to find a babysitter, only 13% reported a need for respite care.

In response to a question about how difficult their adopted child has been to raise, most parents expressed at least some difficulty, but only 12% responded that their child had been very difficult to raise. Their responses are shown in Figure 2.1.

The survey asked parents if they had concerns about how well their child got along in each area of the child's life, and what they thought would help. The survey specified possible responses and left space for open-ended responses. In relation to the child's functioning at home, most parents expressed that they had some concern with which they would like help. Of the 68% who wanted help, the most frequently requested solution was counseling for the child (30%). Table 2.2 reports the specific ratings on services.

Less than 5% of parents viewed their adopted children as having a very negative adjustment at home. This conclusion is based on the low number of negative responses of parents to questions on closeness to child and effect of the child on the family. The significant majority of families accept even those children with significant impairments and problems and perceive the children as at least somewhat attached.

**Figure 2.1**
How Difficult Has This Child Been to Raise?

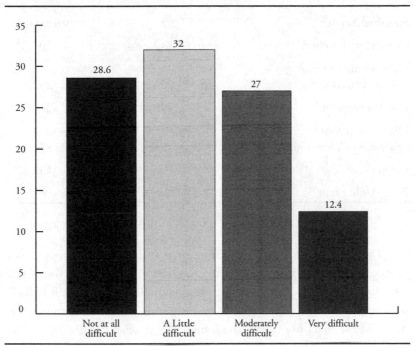

**Child's Adjustment at School**

School adjustment is one of the areas of greatest need for these children and their families. Most children in the survey were in elementary and middle school, as shown in Figure 2.2. Parents reported more concerns related to children's functioning in school than any other area of their lives. When asked to rate the child's overall adjustment in school, compared with other children the same age, parents gave the following responses: 29% excellent, 40% good, 23% fair, and 9% poor. Most parents, however, reported concerns related to their children's struggles at school. Also, 1.6% of children had dropped out of school.

Table 2.3 reports on specific aspects of children's functioning in school, which may be indicative of needs or problems related to school performance. A sizeable percentage (40%) of children receive special education services for learning difficulties. This can be compared to the 2001–2002 school year national average of 13% and the Illinois average of 14.4% of children with individual education plans (National Center for Education Statistics, 2003).

**Table 2.2**
Desired Services to Assist with Child's Adjustment at Home

| Specified Service | n | Percentage |
|---|---|---|
| Counseling for child | 342 | 30 |
| Help learning to manage child's behavior | 284 | 25 |
| Family counseling | 239 | 21 |
| Information about parenting children like mine | 194 | 17 |
| Respite care | 148 | 13 |
| Better child care | 48 | 4 |

For the 26% of children repeating grades, the most common grades repeated were kindergarten and first grade. As the grade level increased, schools held back fewer children. Whereas about 70 students were held back in second and third grades, many fewer repeated grades four through six. About 30 children had repeated junior high or high school grades. Some children had repeated multiple grades, however, ranging up to four for one child.

School suspension or expulsion was a problem for about one-fourth of the children. Many had been suspended or expelled multiple times. For example, of those children experiencing school suspension, 63% had been suspended more than once, ranging up to 20 or more suspensions for four children. Likewise, about half of the children who had been expelled had multiple expulsions, ranging up to 10.

Zill (1994) used data from the National Health Interview Survey on Child Health to make a comparison study of adopted children and children living in other types of families. He reported the number of children who had been suspended or expelled from school as 5% in children living with both birthparents, 6% in adoptive families, and 17% in families headed by unmarried mothers, versus the 25% found in this study.

**Figure 2.2**
Current Grade in School for Children

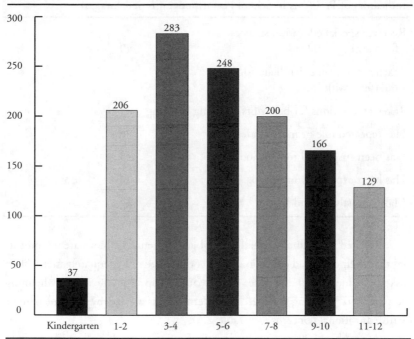

The researchers analyzed grades in school separately for regular and special education students (see Figure 2.3). They excluded four students who received gifted education services from the special education figures, because these children do not have learning problems. Of children, 83% of children were reported to have at least satisfactory grades The study assumed that fewer children in special education would be making poor grades, because their classes would be specifically targeted to their needs. The reverse, however, was true. Of the 216 children making mostly Ds and Fs, 60% were receiving special education services. The grade distributions reported for children are shown in Figure 2.3. A positive finding of this study is that the large majority of children are making satisfactory or better grades in school, and almost half (47.6%) have an A or B average.

Hyperactivity problems were present in a substantial number of children. The researchers incorporated the Connors' scale for hyperactivity into the survey, and Table 2.4 reports on these items.

**Table 2.3**
Indicators of Problems in School Performance (in percentages)

| | |
|---|---|
| Receives special education services for learning problems | 40 |
| Teacher complains that behavior interferes with learning | 54 |
| Takes medications for behaviors affecting learning | 31 |
| Has repeated one or more grades | 26 |
| Has been suspended from school | 25 |
| Has been expelled from school | 6 |
| Makes mostly Ds and Fs | 17 |

Related to children's overall school adjustment, 39% of parents indicated that their child had educational needs that were not adequately met. When asked to identify the services that would help, the most overwhelming response was tutoring for the child, identified as a need by 66% of parents with educational concerns (see Table 2.5).

More than 100 parents made other suggestions about services to help their child with school. Most wanted extra help for subjects the child struggled with, primarily reading. Some whose children were not in special education felt their children needed special education services for learning disabilities or speech and hearing problems. Others suggested specific needs: anger management, an adequate individual educational plan, a more inclusive setting, not being mainstreamed, a therapeutic day school, help with autism, and others. One parent just responded, "I don't know, but he needs help!" A substantial minority of these children and families could use the services of an educational advocate. Some parents' responses indicated that they themselves were knowledgeable advocates for their children's educational needs.

## Children's Physical and Mental Health

The overwhelming majority of children were reported to be in excellent (50%) or good (42%) physical health, with 7% reported as having fair health, and less than 1% poor health.

**Figure 2.3**
Average Grades in School Special Education

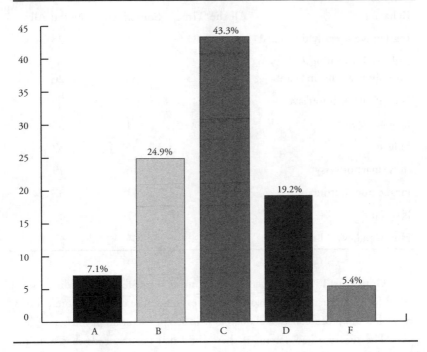

The survey asked parents about the proportion of health costs paid for by themselves, private insurance, and Medicaid. Two-thirds stated that all or almost all of medical costs were paid for by Medicaid, and only 17% did not use Medicaid. Conversely, 69% did not cover any medical costs with private insurance, and 18% used it for all or almost all of medical costs. Of respondents, 39% reported that they themselves paid for some or all of their child's medical costs.

Overall, 29% of parents reported that their child had special medical needs, and 18% reported that their child had a chronic medical problem. For example, one parent stated that her daughter, whom she had raised since infancy, was now a teen and struggled with cystic fibrosis, diabetes, and permanent liver damage. She had failed to thrive as an infant and had extensive health problems from birth onward. This mother has to take her child to a large medical center more than an hour from her home two or three times a week for medical care.

**Table 2.4**
Symptoms of Hyperactivity and Attention Problems (in percentages)

| Behavior | All the Time | Sometimes | Not at All |
|---|---|---|---|
| Inattentive/is easily distracted | 40 | 35 | 25 |
| Fails to finish things/ has short attention span | 39 | 35 | 26 |
| Is excitable or impulsive | 33 | 32 | 36 |
| Is quarrelsome | 27 | 41 | 32 |
| Fidgets | 27 | 36 | 37 |
| Acts smart or sassy | 25 | 46 | 29 |
| Has temper outbursts | 22 | 41 | 37 |
| Is defiant | 21 | 37 | 43 |
| Hums/makes odd noises | 19 | 34 | 47 |

Of parents, 15% had difficulty getting medical care for their children. When asked for recommendations, many parents expressed the need for more dentists, mental health professionals, and doctors who accept Medicaid payments.

The survey asked parents if their child had health needs that were not being met and what they thought would help, and 40% said their children did have unmet health needs. Most parents expressing medical needs specified, "more doctors who take Medicaid card." Other suggested services were: someone to help care for child and provide break (11%), help getting child to the doctor (8%), and special medical equipment (4%).

### Children's Mental Health

Parents generally rated their children's mental health less positively than their physical health. Overall, one in four parents rated their child's mental health as fair (20%) or poor (5%). Most parents, however, rated it as excellent (30%) or good (45%).

Of parents, 53% stated that their children had seen a counselor for emotional or behavioral problems. For those children, slightly more than half had received treatment for emotional or behavioral problems at age 6 or younger.

In addition to parents' overall appraisals of children's mental health, the

**Table 2.5**
Services to Assist with Educational Needs

| Service | n | Percentage |
|---|---|---|
| Tutoring for child | 336 | 66 |
| Afterschool program | 188 | 37 |
| Special testing/evaluation | 161 | 32 |
| Someone to help child get in right kind of class | 141 | 28 |
| Information about how to the best help for the child | 133 | 26 |

survey incorporated a standardized measure of child behavior problems, the Behavior Problem Index (BPI), developed by Peterson and Zill (1986) for use with children age 4 and older. A number of national surveys of children and youth have used this index, which facilitates comparison of the sample group of children to those in the general population.

Primary studies incorporating BPI are the National Health Interview Survey in its Child Health Supplement and the National Longitudinal Survey of Youth (NLSY). The National Center for Health Statistics (NCHS, 1982) conducted the first survey of 15,416 children from birth to age 17 in 1981. The Ohio State University Center for Human Resource Research conducted NLSY (Baker, Keck, Mott, & Quinlan, 1993).

The original BPI contains 28 items evaluated on a three-point scale, however, the scoring for the overall index dichotomizes ratings into yes/no categories. One item (*cries too much*) is omitted on computing the index for children 12 and older. The researchers viewed this item as characteristic of immaturity and more common among younger children. For this analysis, the researchers omitted this item for calculating older children's scores when comparing them with averages in the national child sample. For several reasons, however, the researchers included the item for the overall analysis of adopted children. An item analysis of this variable indicated that parents identified *cries too much* as frequently for older children as younger children. Because parents identified approximately one-third of the children in this sample as developmentally delayed, and because grief and depression are commonly reported difficulties among adopted children, the researchers included this item in the

**Table 2.6**
Behavior Problems Comprising the Behavior Problem Index

| Behavior | Very True or Often True | Somewhat or Sometimes True | Never True |
|---|---|---|---|
| Has difficulty concentrating | 28 | 36 | 36 |
| Is impulsive/acts without thinking | 25 | 37 | 38 |
| Cheats or tell lies | 24 | 44 | 32 |
| Argues too much | 21 | 39 | 40 |
| Demands a lot of attention | 19 | 30 | 51 |
| Has sudden changes in mood or feelings | 18 | 49 | 33 |
| Is restless or overly active/ cannot sit still | 18 | 33 | 49 |
| Is stubborn, sullen, or irritable | 15 | 37 | 48 |
| Has a very strong temper and loses it easily | 15 | 27 | 58 |
| Is high strung, tense, or nervous | 14 | 30 | 56 |
| Does not seem to feel sorry after misbehaving | 14 | 30 | 56 |
| Is disobedient at home | 13 | 46 | 41 |
| Has difficulty getting mind off certain thoughts | 12 | 30 | 58 |
| Is disobedient at school | 11 | 38 | 51 |
| Is easily confused/seems to be in a fog | 11 | 30 | 59 |
| Is too fearful or anxious | 10 | 29 | 61 |
| Has trouble getting along with other children | 9 | 34 | 57 |
| Bullies or is cruel or mean to others | 8 | 28 | 64 |
| Is too dependent on others | 8 | 26 | 65 |
| Has trouble getting along with teachers | 7 | 30 | 63 |
| Feels worthless or inferior | 7 | 29 | 63 |
| Is unhappy, sad, or depressed | 7 | 28 | 65 |
| Clings to adults | 7 | 25 | 68 |
| Breaks thing on purpose/ deliberately destroys things | 7 | 19 | 74 |
| Is not liked by other children | 6 | 30 | 64 |
| Feels or complains that no one loves him or her | 6 | 27 | 67 |
| Cries too much | 6 | 16 | 78 |
| Is withdrawn, does not get involved with others | 5 | 21 | 74 |

overall analysis of BPI. In addition, its inclusion for all children enabled the combining of younger and older children's scores in the overall bivariate and multivariate analyses.

Table 2.6 shows the responses from the current study on individual BPI items. When any BPI item in the scale is left blank, researchers cannot compute an overall score. For children in this study, the researchers could compute total scores for 1,048 children.

The frequencies in Table 2.6 indicate that eight of the listed behavior problems are present in the majority of children in the survey. The most common problems reported are: cheats or tells lies (68%), has sudden changes in mood or feelings (67%), has difficulty concentrating (64%), is impulsive or acts without thinking (62%), argues too much (60%), is disobedient at home (59%), is stubborn, sullen or irritable (52%), and is restless or overly active (51%).

On the overall BPI, the mean score for the adopted children in the survey is 11.91, compared with a mean of 6.44 for a group of more than 11,500 children sampled in the national survey (Zill, Peterson, & Snyder, 1987). Overall, 39% of adopted children's scores were above the 90th percentile of normed scores, and 55% of adopted children fell in the top quartile of normed scores.

Table 2.7 reports BPI scores for children in each percentile level in this sample of adopted children and in the national sample on which the index was normed. For example, to be in the 50th percentile of scores, the children in this study would have a score of 11, whereas children in the national study would have a score of 5. At the upper levels of the distribution, adopted children score 9 to 10 points higher than children in the national sample.

Figure 2.4 depicts the BPI score distributions for children in this study.

## Other Aspects of Mental Health Functioning

A measure of the mental health needs of children is the extent to which their problems require psychiatric or residential placement. A relatively small number of children (6%) had been placed in a psychiatric facility, group home, or residential treatment center after adoption, and 9% were placed prior to adoption. Altogether, 12% of children had been in a psychiatric hospital or residential facility at some point. As might be expected, the reasons for placement, as presented by parents, were very serious. Most parents described oppositional defiant behavior, suicide attempts, specific mental illness, or violence. Many of these parents described children who had some or all of these diffi-

**Table 2.7**

Comparison of Behavior Problem Index Percentile Scores for Adoption Assistance and National Samples

| Percentile | Adopted Sample | National Sample |
|---|---|---|
| 10th | 1 | 0.21 |
| 25th | 4 | 1.71 |
| 50th | 11 | 5.09 |
| 75th | 19 | 9.87 |
| 90th | 24 | 14.83 |
| *M* | 11.91 | 6.44 |
| *n* | 1,024 | 11,588 |

culties. Although these families represent a small percentage of the total, these family difficulties predict serious, ongoing problems. The following statements typify such comments:

> Totally out of control at home. Uncooperative, oppositional defiant behavior/attachment disorder.

> Child continuously causes problems, lies, steals, starts fires, very defiant toward mother. Cannot get along with other children.

> Very defiant, aggressive behavior toward teachers, classmates, parent. [Has] threatened to hurt and/or kill. Totally noncompliant.

> Paranoia, violent aggression, cognitive distortion, thinks world owes him.

> Was homicidal at 5 1/2 years. Many hospitalizations until age 10, went to residential school until 15, then went to young adult program for mentally ill.

> Sexually molested sister. Could not control anger. Set fires. O.D.D. behaviors—destructive.

**Figure 2.4**
Behavior Problem Index Scores

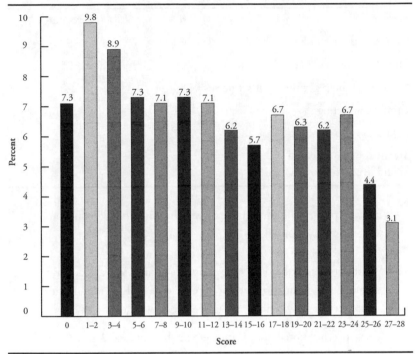

My child was born with drugs, a "drug baby." Teen problems and emotional problems. Dissociative behavior—your worst nightmare, e.g., tried to kill me.

Schizophrenia, schizoaffective.

[My child has] conduct disorder, oppositional defiant disorder, and is sexually aggressive.

Severe depression. She considered jumping from a third floor stair rail at school. She chose not to jump but they asked that she be evaluated.

Impulsive behavior; we feared he was a safety threat. Major depression, ADHD [attention deficit hyperactivity disorder], bipolar.

**Table 2.8**
Services Desired to Meet Mental Health Needs

| Service | n | Percentage |
| --- | --- | --- |
| Counseling for child | 269 | 32 |
| Providers who will take Medicaid | 208 | 25 |
| Someone to help get the right services | 184 | 22 |
| Family counseling | 164 | 20 |
| Support group | 137 | 16 |
| Treatment center where child lives temporarily | 67 | 8 |

He was very sad. Didn't understand why his mom left him and wanted to hurt himself.

We are trying our hardest to keep him at home. Educational environment has been difficult for him. He is in his "last chance" school setting now. This area has been very difficult for all of us.

A few parents noted that improvement had occurred since the child's placement experience. For example, "Since she got older, past 16 years, her behavior got a little out of hand. To get her back on track I had her stay in [a] hospital for two weeks for counseling. It helped a great deal." Another noted,

Since she has been taking Ritalin she is doing lots better. She has improved on all the behavior problems [listed on BPI]. Before Ritalin, I would have rated her 2 [*the behavior was often or very often true*]. Much improvement!!

Another parent described her child hanging out with troubled children, serving detention, sneaking out at night, and having illicit sexual encounters with older girls and boys. The child is now older, however, working hard to do better, and excelling in school.

The survey also assessed alcohol and drug problems. Overall, parents reported that 7.5% of teens had such a problem.

The survey asked parents if their child had mental health needs that were not being met and what services they thought would help. Of parents, 42% reported service needs related to their child's mental health (see Table 2.8).

Parents also gave other suggestions for assisting with their children's mental health needs:

- Placement in treatment center
- One-on-one aid
- Psychiatric care
- Respite
- Counselor with right skills
- Lifeskills classes
- List of providers who take Medicaid
- Therapeutic camp
- Help with teen parenting
- Treatment for attachment disorder
- Evaluation of medications
- Child support group of same sex children
- Help preparing for adulthood
- Therapeutic school
- Parent support group
- Post-traumatic stress disorder counseling

## Children's Adjustment in the Neighborhood and Community

Overall, 22% ($n$ = 294) of parents had concerns about their child's ability to get along in their neighborhood or community. The study explored specific aspects of the children's functioning outside their homes and schools and asked parents to compare their child's abilities on these dimensions with other children the same age (see Table 2.9).

The survey asked parents whether their child had been arrested or in trouble with the police, and 9.5% of children overall had been. When the researchers analyzed teens separately, 20% had been in trouble with the police. The most frequent reason was stealing, followed by assault, running away, and vandalism.

More than 280 parents (21%) wrote specific descriptions of their concerns about their children's functioning in the neighborhood. The researchers

**Table 2.9**
Children's Abilities to Function in their Community (in percentages)

| Ability | Not at All | Poorly | Fairly Well | Very Well |
|---|---|---|---|---|
| Make friends with children of similar age | 2 | 15 | 37 | 46 |
| Get along with children in neighborhood | 2 | 9 | 45 | 44 |
| Choose friends the parents are comfortable with | 5 | 13 | 46 | 36 |
| Make good decisions | 6 | 20 | 43 | 30 |
| Fit in with organized groups | 6 | 13 | 37 | 45 |

subjected these responses to qualitative analysis and categorized them according to themes. The nature of the responses is shown below, with samples given in each category. These themes are reported in order of their frequency, beginning with the most common.

• Child has poor reasoning skills and is easily led astray:

She doesn't understand the difference between right and wrong. She's easily swayed…, so she has to be watched closely.

He wants friends so badly he will go with anyone. He's learning to make better choices.

• Child is generally not accepted by others:

He is friendly, but because of his negative behaviors and being nonverbal, not many people want to be friends.

It is hard for her to be accepted because she is very emotional and acts different.

There is a stigma being a former foster child.

The community is uncomfortable with him.

Because he is delayed, kids won't play with him…he can't keep up with them.

• Child is drawn to friends who are a bad influence:

My child hangs around with and makes friends with children who get into trouble.

He appears to be drawn to troubled children.

Always wants to mingle with the very bad. Wants to follow the leader to prove he is capable to hang out.

• Child cannot get along with others or is a bad influence on others:

She steals, lies, can't get along; wants "revenge" when things don't go her way!

She will push everyone's buttons until they get sick of it.…Child leads others into disobedience and drugs and alcohol.…She is a supplier.

Too attracted to young children, chronic liar. The neighbors either love him or despise him.

• Worry about destructive influences of neighborhood:

My concerns are about the gangs and the drug dealers.

She is biracial in a white neighborhood and sometimes is [an] object of racism and bigotry, causing me to fear for her safety.

• Child has difficulty trusting or attaching:

He has no feelings about being connected to family, school, or community, so he has no reservations about stealing from or lying to others.

He doesn't trust very many people.

## Suggested Solutions

Parents' service needs regarding the children's adjustments in the community, in order of frequency, were:

- Counseling
- Recreational programs
- Safer neighborhoods.
- Support groups
- Aid for transition to adulthood
- Respite, not only for parents, but for children to have time away from very troubled siblings
- Child care, particularly afterschool care, help for single parents, or help with children who, despite being older, could not be safely left alone
- Residential care
- Tutoring
- Mentors, especially male role models
- Transportation
- Child's medication needs, including finding the right medication and help gaining child compliance with medication regimens
- Special information for parents, such as how to raise a child who has been severely neglected or meeting the needs of a child with severe anger problems

## Resources and Services

Most families will manage the challenges of raising their children using their own resources and those in their communities. For families adopting children with histories of maltreatment, services may be even more important. The survey asked parents to check the types of supportive services the family had used after adoption and rate their helpfulness, and 1,086 responded (see Table 2.10). In addition, parents described other services they had used.

Overall, 66% of parents reported using at least one service. Of those using services, the mean number of services per respondent was 3.2. Some families reported using services beyond those listed. Parents identified specialized treatment most commonly, such as consultation with an expert in fetal alcohol syndrome, services for attachment disorders, or intervention related to

**Table 2.10**
Services Used and Rating of Helpfulness

| | | | Degree of Helpfulness | | |
|---|---|---|---|---|---|
| Service | Percentage | n | Not | Somewhat | Very |
| Child counseling | 44 | 486 | 9 | 47 | 44 |
| Family/parent counseling | 32 | 352 | 6 | 52 | 41 |
| Adoption assistance worker | 22 | 246 | 10 | 53 | 37 |
| Parent support group | 21 | 228 | 17 | 49 | 34 |
| Original agency | 15 | 163 | 23 | 48 | 29 |
| Programs/seminars on adoption | 15 | 160 | 16 | 61 | 23 |
| Other Department of Family and Children's Services worker | 14 | 152 | 17 | 52 | 31 |
| Child support group | 13 | 140 | 26 | 46 | 29 |
| Out-of-home placement | 12 | 129 | 21 | 50 | 29 |

ADHD. A close second was the support of church, friends, or family, or other nonagency support. Parents also mentioned education-related services and training or information on special topics.

## Barriers

Parents reported problems getting help in 46% of cases. Again, parents chose from a list of possible barriers. Table 2.11 reports their responses. Parents identified other problems in 4% of cases. These covered a broad range. The most common responses were ineffective or nonspecialized counseling and finding optometrists that accept the medical card.

In addition to general barriers to finding and using services, parents identified specific services they have had trouble getting for their children. The majority (58%) reported such difficulty (see Table 2.12).

When parents listed needed services beyond those in Table 2.12, they mirrored earlier responses on service barriers. Getting needed medical services, particularly eyeglasses, braces, and dental care, were the most commonly

**Table 2.11**
Barriers to Receiving Services

| Barrier | *n* | Percentage |
|---|---|---|
| Dentists do not accept medical card | 395 | 33 |
| Doctors do not accept medical card | 301 | 25 |
| Do not know how to find available services | 200 | 17 |
| Counselors do not accept medical card | 171 | 14 |
| Services are too far away from where we live | 157 | 13 |
| Cannot find kind of services child/family needs | 154 | 13 |
| Services do not exist in my community | 145 | 12 |
| Have to wait too long to receive services | 136 | 11 |
| Services needed are too expensive | 115 | 10 |
| Helping professionals do not understand adoption | 109 | 9 |
| Services are too brief | 78 | 7 |
| Eligibility requirements | 63 | 5 |
| Do not trust information will be confidential | 61 | 5 |
| Professionals do not understand race/culture | 30 | 3 |

cited difficulties by far. Education-related problems followed. These included getting children evaluated for special education in a timely manner and finding tutors. Parents mentioned special child care, including before- and after-school care and child care for older children who cannot be left alone. Two mothers had had serious illnesses and needed child care for the time they were hospitalized. Some parents noted specialized counseling or mental health services as well.

**Table 2.12**
Specific Service or Resource Difficulties

| Service | n | Percentage |
|---|---|---|
| Counseling | 159 | 13 |
| Special education | 134 | 11 |
| Child care | 128 | 11 |
| Respite care | 128 | 11 |
| Medical care | 120 | 10 |
| General school services | 89 | 7 |
| Residential care | 45 | 4 |

Parents listed the need for diagnostic evaluations and specialized interventions related to uncommon disorders. Finally, a few parents mentioned material needs, such as help with the cost of school uniforms, adult diapers for disabled children, or a wheelchair.

### Effect of Adoption on Family Relationships

In addition to children's adjustment, the study explored the effect of adoption on family relationships through questions related to perceived closeness in the parent-child relationship and the effect of the child's adoption on the relationship with the respondent's spouse or partner, if applicable, and the overall family. A very small percentage of parents said they did not feel close to their child or reported an overall negative effect of the adoption on their family. A somewhat higher percentage, however, perceived the adopted child as having weakened their marital relationship (see Table 2.13). In cases in which children were judged as having a more negative effect on the family, it was most often a negative effect on the spousal relationship.

## Summary

Children in this study adjusted well to life in their adoptive families. They generally fared well in school and the community, but in these areas, parents

**Table 2.13**
Dynamics of Adopted Child and Family

| Question | Percentage |
|---|---|
| **How close do you feel to your child?** | |
| Very close | 83 |
| Somewhat | 15 |
| Not at all | 2 |
| **Effect of child on spousal relationship?** | |
| No effect | 44 |
| Strengthened | 43 |
| Weakened | 114 |
| **How has adoption affected the family?** | |
| Very positively | 44 |
| Positively | 28 |
| Mixed | 24 |
| Negatively | 3 |
| Very negatively | 1 |

reported less positive adjustment. Although most children received satisfactory grades, more than half had behaviors that interfered with learning, 40% were receiving special education services, and a surprising 25% had been suspended or expelled. Parents reported that most children were in good or excellent health. Their mental health was rated less positively, with 25% of children rated fair or poor in mental health functioning.

Perhaps most important, children in this study were in families where they were valued and cared for. Their parents reported feeling close to them and that their adoptions had a positive effect on the family. Parents would choose to adopt their children again, even knowing everything they now know.

# References

Baker, P. C., Keck, C. K., Mott, F. L., & Quinlan, S. V. (1993). *NLSY child handbook, revised edition: A guide to the 1986-1990 National Longitudinal Survey of Youth Child Data*. Columbus, OH: Center for Human Resource Research, Ohio State University.

National Center for Education Statistics. (2003). *Overview of public elementary and secondary schools and districts: School year 2001–2002*. Available from http://nces.ed.gov/pubs2003/overview2003/.

National Center for Health Statistics. (1982). Current estimates from the National Health Interview Survey: United States, 1981 (DHHS Pub. No. [PHS] 83-1569). *Vital and Health Statistics*. Washington, DC: U.S. Government Printing Office.

Peterson, J. L., & Zill, N. (1986). Marital disruption, parent-child relationships, and behavioral problems in children. *Journal of Marriage and the Family, 48*, 295–307.

Zill, N., Peterson, J. L., & Snyder, N. O. (1987). *Analysis of public use data from 1981 Child Health Supplement to the National Health Interview Survey*. Washington, DC: Child Trends.

Zill, N. (1994). *Adopted children in the United States: A profile based on a national survey of child health*. Washington, DC: Child Trends.

# CHAPTER THREE

# Measures of Overall Adoption Adjustment

Several survey questions assessed various aspects of the overall adoption adjustment of the child and family. The researchers explored these questions individually and analyzed the relationship of these measures to other factors. With a sample as large as this one, modest differences in distribution will result in statistically significant associations.

The analysis reports the mean BPI score for each variable assessing overall adoption outcome. This depicts the relationship between the severity of children's behavior problems and other aspects of adoption adjustment. For each of these variables, the BPI score is very strongly statistically related to the level of parents' responses.

## Parental Attitudes About Adoption*

Several questions explored parents' attitudes toward their adoption of the child. On these questions, parents' positive responses varied in intensity, but a very small minority of parents gave negative responses. Their responses, which Tables 3.1 and 3.2 detail, indicate an overwhelming acceptance of adopted children and satisfaction with the adoption of these children. Each question about parental attitudes toward adoption is discussed in the following, along with the significance test between this variable and children's BPI scores.

---

\*     In the following text, degrees of freedom are not reported, but can be discerned on most analyses from the data presented in the tables.

**Table 3.1**
How Satisfied Are You with Your Adoption Experience?

| Response | Percentage | n | BPI Score |
|---|---|---|---|
| Very satisfied | 59 | 610 | 9.44 |
| Satisfied | 32 | 337 | 14.26 |
| Negative or very negative | 9 | 88 | 19.61 |

Note. BPI = Behavior Problem Index. rho = .38; $p < .001$.

Another question asked whether parents would recommend adoption to others. Only 5% responded negatively to this question, with 12% being unsure, and 82% giving a positive response.

In addition to lower levels of child behavior problems, parental satisfaction with adoption was associated with the following: younger age of the child (rho = .15, $p < .001$), fewer adverse conditions in the child's background ($r = .20$, $p < .001$), lower income (rho = .16, $p < .001$), and being a single parent ($\chi^2 = 10.07$, $p < .01$). Rosenthal and Groze (1991) also found more positive outcomes among single parents.

The only child disabilities or special needs that are related to parental dissatisfaction are emotional disturbance ($\chi^2 = 116.55$, $p < .001$), behavior problems ($\chi^2 = 119.38$, $p < .001$), and learning disabilities ($\chi^2 = 16.87$, $p < .001$). Physical handicaps, mental retardation, chronic medical problems, and developmental delays are not associated with parental dissatisfaction.

The child's being perceived as having a negative effect on the marriage is strongly associated with dissatisfaction ($\chi^2 = 153.30$, $p < .001$). For example, the level of dissatisfaction was seven times greater for those who felt the adoption had a negative effect on their marriage than for those who did not. This may be a reason for the relationship between single parent families and more positive responses.

Age at placement also was associated with parental satisfaction. Parents of children placed at age 3 or younger reported higher levels of satisfaction than those with children placed at older ages ($\chi^2 = 14.00$, $p < .01$).

Difficulty in raising the child and satisfaction are very strongly linked ($\chi^2 = 403.49$, $p < .001$). For those who said the child was not at all difficult

**Table 3.2**
Would You Adopt This Child Again?

| Response | Percentage | n | BPI Score |
|---|---|---|---|
| Yes, definitely | 76 | 792 | 10.30 |
| Probably would adopt | 17 | 161 | 16.39 |
| Probably not or definitely not | 7 | 73 | 18.73 |

Note. BPI = Behavior Problem Index. rho = .35; $p < .001$.

to raise, the dissatisfaction rate was less than 1%, compared with 40% for those children rated as very difficult to raise.

In addition, parental satisfaction is related to type of adoption (chi-square = 47.26, $p < .001$). Very few relatives report being dissatisfied (4.5%), whereas 14% (1 in 7) of matched parents are dissatisfied. Also, those with more than one adopted child report slightly higher levels of satisfaction ($\chi^2$ = 8.12, $p < .05$).

## Effect of Adoption on Family

Responses on two questions that explored the effect of adoption on the family and on the parents' marriage, if applicable, are reported in Tables 3.3 and 3.4. Parental responses on these questions are strongly associated with the level of child behavior problems.

Perceiving a negative effect of the adoption on the family as a whole is very rare. This finding is similar to those of other studies using this question. For example, Rosenthal and Groze's (1992) survey of more than 700 families found an overall negative response of 4%, which is the same percentage found in this study. In Groze's (1996) later study, only 3% identified the adoption as having a negative effect on their family during the first survey, but at follow-up four years later, 14% responded in this manner.

Less positive responses about effect of the child on the family are associated with children whose adoptive parent had a change in marital status since their adoption ($\chi^2$ = 19.16, $p < .001$). Also, single parents give more positive responses on this question than parents from two-parent families ($\chi^2$ = 23.38, $p < .001$).

**Table 3.3**
How Has Adoption Affected Your Family?

| Response | Percentage | n | BPI Score |
|---|---|---|---|
| Very positively/positively | 72 | 741 | 9.60 |
| Mixed, both positive and negative | 24 | 243 | 17.49 |
| Negative or very negative | 4 | 44 | 20.93 |

Note. BPI = Behavior Problem Index. rho = .48; $p < .001$.

**Table 3.4**
Has Adoption of This Child Strengthened or Weakened Your Marriage?

| Response | Percentage | n | BPI Score |
|---|---|---|---|
| Strengthened the relationship | 45 | 319 | 10.92 |
| Had no effect | 41 | 293 | 11.22 |
| Weakened the relationship | 14 | 103 | 19.11 |

Note. BPI = Behavior Problem Index. rho = .23; $p < .001$.

Children of parents who felt that their child had a negative effect on their marriage had experienced more maltreatment and preplacement adverse conditions ($r = .16$, $p < .001$).

## Attachment in the Parent-Child Relationship

The survey asked parents about their closeness to their adopted child and their child's ability to give and receive affection, which the researchers used as a proxy for attachment. Tables 3.5 and 3.6 report responses on these items and the corresponding BPI mean scores.

A child's maltreatment history affects child/parent closeness. Children who have problems giving and receiving affection have a greater frequency of each type of maltreatment or adverse preplacement condition, particularly physical abuse, as shown in Table 3.7. For example, the frequency of attachment problems is three times greater for physically abused children than for

**Table 3.5**
How Close Do You Feel to Your Child?

| Response | Percentage | n | BPI Score |
|---|---|---|---|
| Very close | 82 | 855 | 10.64 |
| Somewhat close | 16 | 167 | 17.49 |
| Not at all close | 2 | 23 | 19.61 |

Note. BPI = Behavior Problem Index. rho = .33; $p < .001$.

**Table 3.6**
How Well Is Your Child Able to Give and Receive Affection?

| Response | Percentage | n | BPI Score |
|---|---|---|---|
| Very well | 58 | 600 | 8.66 |
| Fairly well | 30 | 316 | 15.27 |
| Poorly or not at all | 12 | 125 | 18.98 |

Note. BPI = Behavior Problem Index. rho = $-.47$; $p < .001$.

those who did not experience physical abuse. Parents' level of closeness to their children is associated with each type of maltreatment and adverse preplacement condition. In addition, a greater number of adverse conditions occurring in the child's life prior to placement is associated with more attachment problems in the parent-child relationship ($\chi^2 = 64.03$, $p < .001$).

Attachment problems are associated with behavior problems, emotional disturbance, and learning disabilities, but not with other types of disabilities or special needs.

Although a very small percentage of children are reported as having difficulty in giving and receiving affection, the percentage of these problems is greatest in matched adoptions (16%). Of foster parent adopters, 13% report these difficulties, and only 8% of relative adopters do. Also, single parents report fewer problems in children's attachment to the parent than two-parent families ($\chi^2 = 7.94$, $p < .05$).

**Table 3.7**

Factors Associated with Attachment Problems

| Variable | Chi-Square | Significance Level |
| --- | --- | --- |
| Physical abuse | 50.08 | *** |
| Sexual abuse | 26.85 | *** |
| Serious neglect | 16.17 | *** |
| Two or more foster homes | 27.95 | *** |
| Prenatal substance exposure | 22.37 | *** |
| Number of adverse conditions | 85.98 | *** |
| Behavior problems | 170.68 | *** |
| Emotional disturbance | 148.56 | *** |
| Learning disabilities | 25.06 | *** |
| Type of adoption | 24.06 | ** |
| Two-parent family | 7.94 | * |

$*p < .05.$ $**p < .01.$ $***p < .001.$

Parents whose children have attachment problems are more likely to view the child as having a negative effect on their marriage or the family as a whole. Also, the child's ability to give and receive affection is strongly related to parents' feeling close to their children ($\chi^2 = 474.79$, $p < .001$). For example, those who rated their children as having difficulty giving and receiving affection were seven times more likely than other parents to respond "not at all" on how close they were to their child.

In summary, all measures of overall adoption adjustment are strongly related to the level of child behavior problems. More positive responses on overall measures also are associated with younger age of the child, fewer adverse conditions in the child's background, lower income families, and being a single parent. In addition, parental satisfaction is related to children's being placed prior to age 3, the child's not being perceived as difficult to raise, and the type of adoption. The level of parent-child attachment is strongly linked to child experiences of maltreatment and other adverse conditions as well as the number of adverse conditions experienced by the child.

**Table 3.8**
Adversities Associated with Level of Behavior Problems

| Variable | Spearman's rho |
|---|---|
| Physical abuse | .30 |
| Sexual abuse | .29 |
| Prenatal substance exposure | .29 |
| Two or more foster homes | .22 |
| Serious neglect | .18 |
| Back/forth between home and care | .16 |
| Psychiatric/residential treatment center before placement | .15 |
| In adoptive home before placement | .14 |

Note. $p < .001$.

## Level of Child's Adjustment

The primary measure of overall adjustment of the child is the BPI score. As discussed throughout this analysis, a higher level of behavior problems is associated with negative outcomes in all other areas. A number of other variables were associated with the severity of child behavior problems. One of the strongest predictors of higher behavior problems is the number of adverse conditions children experienced prior to adoptive placement ($rho = .35$, $p < .001$).

Also, each adverse condition listed is related to behavior problem severity (see Table 3.8). These are presented in order of their strength of association. It is important to reiterate that many parents were uncertain as to their child's previous experiences, so that children could actually have had these experiences and not be identified as such.

The special needs or disabilities of the child that relate to greater severity of behavior problems are: emotional disturbance ($rho = .52$, $p < .001$), learning disabilities ($rho = .33$, $p < .001$), developmental delays ($rho = .27$, $p < .27$), and chronic medical problems ($rho = .11$, $p < .001$).

**Table 3.9**
Association of Child's Race and Behavior Problems

| Race | n | BPI Score |
|------|---|-----------|
| African American | 480 | 10.39 |
| Hispanic | 62 | 11.08 |
| White | 357 | 14.08 |
| Biracial | 58 | 12.67 |

Note. BPI = Behavior Problem Index. chi-square = 61.64; p < .001.

Higher behavior problem scores are associated with younger age of the parent (r = −.13, $p$ < .001), families with higher income (rho = .11, $p$ < .001), and a two-parent family (rho = .12, $p$ < .001). Also, boys have higher behavior problem scores than girls (rho = −.13, $p$ < .001).

Race of the child also is associated with children's BPI scores, with white children having a higher level of behavior problems than children of any other race. White children have a mean score of 14.1 compared with a mean of 11.9 for all other children ($t$ = 2.63, $p$ < .01). African American children have the lowest BPI scores of racial groups. The mean BPI scores for children by race are reported in Table 3.9.

Other studies on racial differences in child welfare adoptees have reported that minority children in general have fewer behavior problems than their white counterparts. For example, Rosenthal and Groze (1992) reported that parents of minority children (73% African American) reported fewer behavior problems among their children. Also, minority children were less likely to have been sexually abused or institutionalized than white children in their study. Pinderhughes' (1998) study of adoptive placements of older children also reported a higher level of social competence and fewer behavior problems for African American than for white children. In a study of adult transracial and same-race adoptees, the most problematic outcomes were found among white males (Brooks & Barth, 1999).

In addition to racial differences, there were significant differences in BPI scores of children who were transracially placed compared with those placed

**Table 3.10**
Age at Removal

| Age | n | Mean BPI Score |
|---|---|---|
| Younger than 1 year | 346 | 11.87 |
| 1–3 years | 273 | 13.25 |
| 4–6 years | 192 | 12.24 |
| 7 or older | 80 | 10.99 |

in a family of the same race ($t$ = 2.61, $p$ < .01). Children placed transracially had a mean BPI score of 13.74, compared with 11.91 for children who were not transracially placed. These differences are even greater when African American children placed in same-race families are compared with African American children transracially placed. This difference is maintained even when controlling for relative placement. Among the children in this study, the 73 African American children transracially placed had a mean BPI score of 14.4. The 407 African American children in same-race homes not placed with relatives have a mean score of 9.9 ($t$ = –4.47, $p$ < .001). Those children who parents identified as biracial are not included in this comparison.

Most other outcome responses (closeness to the child, satisfaction with the adoption, effect of the child on the family) were not significantly different for transracially placed children. Parents were more likely, however, to rate these children as more difficult to raise than children placed in same-race families (chi-square = 24.32, $p$ < .001). There were more transracially placed children rated as moderately difficult to raise, as opposed to a little or not at all difficult.

In addition, age at removal from birthfamily and age at placement are related to behavior problem severity. Children's mean scores according to age ranges on these variables are reported in Tables 3.10 and 3.11. Children removed between ages 1 and 3 had a significantly higher level of behavior problems than children removed at other ages ($t$ = 2.63, $p$ < .01). In addition, children placed in their adoptive homes between the ages of 4 and 6 had behavior problem scores higher than children placed at other ages ($t$ = 2.65, $p$ < .01).

One explanation for the higher level of problems among children removed at ages 1 to 3 and placed at ages 4 to 6 is that these children had

**Table 3.11**
Age at Placement

| Age | n | Mean BPI Score |
|---|---|---|
| Younger than 1 year | 258 | 11.20 |
| 1–3 years | 265 | 12.18 |
| 4–6 years | 215 | 13.32 |
| 7 or older | 178 | 12.63 |

**Table 3.12**
How Does Child Feel about Being Adopted?

| Response | Percentage | n | BPI Score |
|---|---|---|---|
| Feels positive | 72 | 729 | 10.11 |
| Both positive and negative | 26 | 263 | 16.37 |
| Feels negative | 2 | 19 | 20.84 |

Note. rho = .35; $p < .001$.

**Table 3.13**
How Difficult Has Your Child Been to Raise?

| Response | Percentage | n | BPI Score |
|---|---|---|---|
| Not at all difficult | 29 | 303 | 4.96 |
| A little difficult | 31 | 326 | 11.30 |
| Moderately difficult | 28 | 290 | 15.97 |
| Very difficult | 12 | 123 | 21.28 |

Note. BPI = Behavior Problem Index. rho = .65; $p < .001$.

**Table 3.14**
Child's Current Age and Difficulty in Raising

| Age | Percentage Rated as Very Difficult | Mean BPI Score |
|---|---|---|
| 8 or younger | 7.4% | 11.58 |
| 9–11 | 7.6 | 11.29 |
| 12–14 | 13.3 | 12.14 |
| 15–17 | 19.4 | 13.14 |
| 18 or older | 31.2 | 12.58 |

Note. BPI = Behavior Problem Index.

interrupted attachments and ongoing impermanence at a very young age, but had formed some attachment to a birthfamily. They were at an age when they were very dependent on parents and unable to understand changes in caregivers. Those children in this study who were removed at age 7 or older had the lowest behavior problem scores. This finding corresponds with Howe's (1997) study in England, which found that children with adequate beginnings with their birthfamilies who were removed later in life had many fewer problems than those removed due to adverse treatment at earlier ages.

Another measure of the child's adjustment is the parent's perception of how the child feels about being adopted. Although parents may not always have an accurate perception of children's feelings, this variable was an attempt to assess children's feelings about adoption. As with other outcome variables, the response levels vary significantly with levels of child behavior problems, as reported in Table 3.12.

A final measure of overall adjustment of the child was the question, "In general, how difficult has your child been to raise?" Overall, parents assessed 12% of children as "very difficult." Parents' ratings on the difficulty in raising child question are given in Table 3.13 along with the mean BPI score of children receiving that rating. As might be expected, the level of child behavior problems is strongly associated with parents' judgments of child difficulty.

**Table 3.15**
Adverse Preplacement Conditions Among Children Rated as
Very Difficult and Not Very/Somewhat Difficult (in percentages)

| Variable | Very Difficult | Not Very/ Somewhat Difficult | Significance Level |
|---|---|---|---|
| Physically abused | 49 | 30 | *** |
| Sexually abused | 26 | 15 | *** |
| Seriously neglected | 74 | 61 | *** |
| Exposed to alcohol or drugs before birth | 63 | 59 | ns |
| In two or more foster homes prior to adoption | 52 | 35 | *** |
| In psychiatric treatment center before adoption | 21 | 7 | *** |
| Placed in another adoptive home | 25 | 13 | *** |

***$p < .001$.

## What Factors Differentiate Children Who Are Very Difficult to Raise from the Other Children in this Group?

Child and family functioning is a multidimensional phenomenon, and it is hard to single out one variable as a measure of positive or negative adjustment. Of all the outcome questions asked of parents, the "difficult to raise" question seems to best capture the level of parenting stress connected to parenting a child with special needs. These are the children and parents who are really struggling and are most in need of services. Therefore, these children were compared with the remaining children on all variables to determine which variables seem to truly differentiate this group.

Parents' rating of children as very difficult varied significantly with the current age of the child ($\chi^2 = 87.22$, $p < .001$). "Very difficult" ratings were lowest for young children and increased somewhat with age. The total BPI

**Table 3.16**
Special Needs and Problems of Children Rated as Very Difficult and Not
Very/Somewhat Difficult (in percentages)

| Variable | Very Difficult | Not Very/ Somewhat Difficult | Significance Level |
|---|---|---|---|
| Has learning disability | 68 | 45 | *** |
| Has emotional disturbance | 76 | 30 | *** |
| Has behavior problems | 91 | 46 | *** |
| Has behavior problems rated by parent as severe | 56 | 9 | *** |
| Has difficulty handling anger/frustration | 87 | 31 | *** |
| Has difficulty giving and receiving affection | 38 | 8 | *** |
| Is defiant "all of the time" | 71 | 14 | *** |
| Cheats or tells lies "all of the time" | 70 | 17 | *** |
| Does not feel sorry after misbehaving | 81 | 39 | *** |
| Has trouble getting along with other children | 88 | 36 | *** |
| Is often impulsive/ acts without thinking | 73 | 19 | *** |
| Has difficulty with obsessive thoughts | 75 | 37 | *** |
| Severe rating on problems controlling temper | 58 | 9 | *** |
| Unhappy, sad, or depressed | 81 | 29 | *** |
| Has been suspended from school | 49 | 22 | *** |
| Has alcohol or drug problems | 13 | 2 | *** |

***$p < .001$.

**Table 3.17**
Other Characteristics of Children and Families, for Children Rated as Very Difficult and Not Very/Somewhat Difficult (in percentages)

| Variable | Very Difficult | Not Very/ Somewhat Difficult | Significance Level |
|---|---|---|---|
| Relative adoption | 19 | 42 | *** |
| Matched adoption | 24 | 12 | *** |
| Male child | 62 | 49 | ** |
| Child is African American | 38 | 56 | *** |
| Child is white | 49 | 28 | *** |
| Parent is fully prepared to adopt | 29 | 63 | *** |
| Child needs services not included in subsidy | 64 | 34 | *** |
| Child had negative effect on marriage | 44 | 10 | *** |
| Parent has difficulty finding sitter for child | 87 | 37 | *** |
| Parent wants respite care | 40 | 9 | *** |
| Child was in psychiatric treatment center since adoption | 29 | 3 | *** |
| Child has been in trouble with police | 34 | 6 | *** |
| Child receives special education services | 64 | 37 | *** |
| Parent is dissatisfied with adoption | 40 | 5 | *** |

$**p < .01.$ $***p < .001.$

scores, however, were not associated with age. The percentages of those rated "very difficult" by age groups are listed in Table 3.14, along with mean BPI scores for that age group.

African American children were much less likely to be rated "very difficult" and white children significantly more likely to receive this rating. Tables 3.15, 3.16, and 3.17 report the frequencies of responses on some of the most interesting dimensions, along with the significance level resulting from chi-square tests of difference.

This "very difficult" group of children contains children with complex problems. Most have difficult behavior problems and other special needs, such as chronic medical problems, developmental disabilities, and for some, physical handicaps. Despite these problems, many of these parents are very committed and attached to their children. Half of these children are rated as having an excellent or good adjustment at home, although 59% have unmet educational needs and 90% have seen a counselor for emotional or behavioral problems. Thus, it is important to recognize that a child's being very difficult to raise is not equivalent to lack of parental attachment or commitment.

## References

Brooks, D., & Barth, R. P. (1999). Adult transracial and inracial adoptees: Effects of race, gender, adoptive family structure, and placement history on adjustment outcomes. *American Journal of Orthopsychiatry, 69*(1), 87–99.

Groze, V. (1996). *Successful adoptive families: A longitudinal study of special needs adoption.* Westport, CT: Praeger.

Howe, D. (1997). Parent-reported problems in 211 adopted children: Some risk and protective factors. *Journal of Child Psychology and Psychiatry, 38*, 401–411.

Pinderhughes, E. E. (1998). Short term placement outcomes for children adopted after age five. *Children & Youth Services Review, 20*, 223–249.

Rosenthal, J. A., & Groze, V. K. (1991). Behavioral problems of special needs adopted children. *Children & Youth Services Review, 13*, 343–361.

Rosenthal, J. A., & Groze, V. K. (1992). *Special-needs adoption: A study of intact families.* Westport, CT: Praeger.

# CHAPTER FOUR

# Analysis of Risk and Protective Factors Influencing Child Behavior Problems

The strong relationship between the level of child behavior problems and other aspects of adoption adjustment discussed in Chapter Three shows the importance of minimizing child behavior problems to facilitate positive adjustment for children and families. To learn more about what factors create a high risk of behavior problems among these children, the researchers performed stepwise multiple regression analyses using the BPI score as the criterion. They grouped predictive factors into the conceptual categories of child factors and parent factors and performed hierarchical multiple-regression analyses to determine the significant predictors within each category, and when the two categories are combined. Through regression analyses, researchers can identify the factors that are most important in influencing the level of children's behavior problems.

The child factors included in the first regression analysis were: age at removal (younger than 1, 1–3, 4–6, older than 7), being younger than 3 at adoptive placement, prenatal alcohol or drug exposure, physical abuse, sexual abuse, neglect, having more than one foster home placement, moving back and forth between birthfamily and foster care, race (white, African American, Hispanic), gender, and child's ability to give and receive affection (poorly or not at all vs. fairly well or very well).

## Child Factors Predicting Level of Behavior Problems

Table 4.1 summarizes the first regression equation on child factors predicting level of behavior problems and includes six predictors of the level of child

**Table 4.1**

Child Factors that Best Predict Level of Child Behavior Problems

| Variable | $B$ | $SE$ | Beta | $t$ | Significance Level |
|---|---|---|---|---|---|
| Child | | | | | |
| Had prenatal substance exposure | 4.383 | 0.78 | .248 | 5.605 | .000 |
| Can give and receive affection | −5.543 | 1.22 | −.201 | −4.542 | .000 |
| Is white | 2.355 | 0.77 | .133 | 3.047 | .002 |
| Was sexually abused | 2.911 | 1.01 | .133 | 2.893 | .004 |
| Is female | −1.591 | 0.72 | −.096 | −2.205 | .028 |
| Moved between birthfamily and foster care | 2.026 | 1.03 | .088 | 1.971 | .049 |

Note. $F$ = 19.581; $p$ < .0001; $R$ = .465; $R^2$ = .217; Adjusted $R^2$ = .206.

behavior problems. Taken together, these factors account for 22% of the variation in children's behavior problem scores. The Beta weights of the multiple regression analysis indicate that the most powerful risk factor predicting a high level of behavior problems is prenatal alcohol or drug exposure. Being prenatally exposed to drugs or alcohol increased a child's BPI score by 4.4 points.

The strongest protective factor predicting more positive adjustment was the child's ability to give and receive affection. Being able to give and receive affection decreased a child's BPI score by 5.5 points. Being a girl predicts a more positive adjustment, and being white predicts a higher level of behavior problems. Also, a sexual abuse history and moving back and forth between their birthfamily and other placements predict higher behavior problem scores.

This model is able to predict as much as an 18.8-point span in children's BPI scores (the difference between a child with all the risk factors but none of

**Figure 4.1**
Predicted Highest and Lowest Behavior Problem Index (BPI) Scores

**Highest BPI**

12.4   + 4.4(1)  - 5.5(0)  + 2.4(1)  + 2.9(1)  - 1.6 (0) + 2.0(1)  = 24.1
Constant Drug-    Gives/    Race    Sexually  Gender    BF
            exposed receives affect        abused

**Lowest BPI**

12.4   + 4.4(0)  - 5.5(1)  + 2.4(0)  + 2.9(0)  - 1.6(1)   + 2.0(0)  =   5.3
Constant Drug-    Gives/    Race    Sexually  Gender    BF
            exposed receives affect        abused

Note. BF = Back and forth between home and foster care. 1= factor is present, 0 = factor is not present.

the protective factors, and a child with all the protective factors but none of the risk factors). For example, the predicted scores in Figure 4.1 show the highest and lowest BPI scores predicted by this regression equation.

To translate the figures showing the predictive models for the worst and best case scenarios, the highest BPI score predicted by these seven factors would be a white boy who does not give and receive affection or does so poorly. He experienced alcohol or drug exposure before birth, sexual abuse prior to adoptive placement, and was bounced back and forth between his birthfamily and other placements prior to his adoption. Based on the six factors, this child would have a BPI score of 24.1.

The best case scenario predicted by the model is an African American girl who gives and receives affection fairly well or very well. She did not experience prenatal substance exposure or any sexual abuse. She was not moved back and forth between her birthfamily and foster care. Her score on the BPI is 5.3.

## Parent Factors Predicting Level of Behavior Problems

The researchers performed a second regression analysis on parental factors predicting child behavior problems. The factors included in the analysis were: parent needs services not included in subsidy, race of respondent (white, African American, Hispanic), education level (less than high school, high

**Table 4.2**
Parent Factors Predicting Level of Behavior Problems

| Variable | B | SE | Beta | t | Significance Level |
|---|---|---|---|---|---|
| Parent | | | | | |
| Was fully prepared for adoption | −2.961 | .56 | −.177 | −5.339 | .000 |
| Is white | 3.771 | .53 | .227 | 7.080 | .000 |
| Needs services not in subsidy | 3.751 | .55 | .218 | 6.883 | .000 |
| Completed college | −1.266 | .56 | −.072 | −2.260 | .024 |

Note. $F = 41.272$; $p < .0001$; $R = .396$; $R^2 = .157$; Adjusted $R^2 = .153$.

school, college or beyond), type of adoption (relative, foster, matched), income (less than $25,000, $25,000–$44,999, more than $45,000), change in marital status since adoption, and being fully prepared for adoption. Four parent factors entered the regression equation as predictors of the level of child behavior problems: being fully prepared for adoption, being white, needing services not included in subsidy, and having completed college. Together, these variables account for 16% of the variance in children's behavior problems scores. Table 4.2 summarizes the final regression equation on parent factors.

Table 4.2 indicates that being fully prepared for adoption is the strongest protective factor for predicting positive child adjustment, and the parent's having completed college also enters as a protective factor. The loading of college completion as a protective factor was somewhat surprising, given that higher income generally is associated with a higher rate of problems in studies of child welfare adoptions. Analysis by type of adoption reveals that this effect is attributable to relative adoptions, in which higher education acts as a protective factor. This result is not found among foster or matched adoptive families. Parental risk factors for higher levels of child behavior problems include being white and needing services not included in the child's subsidy agreement.

**Table 4.3**
Combined Child and Parent Predictors of Level of Behavior Problems

| Variable | B | SE | Beta | t | Significance Level |
|---|---|---|---|---|---|
| Parent is white | 3.588 | 0.68 | .214 | 5.282 | .000 |
| Child can give and receive affection | −5.451 | 1.07 | −.199 | −5.108 | .000 |
| Parent needs services not in subsidy | 2.894 | 0.69 | .166 | 4.193 | .000 |
| Child was sexually abused | 4.185 | 0.89 | .186 | 4.409 | .000 |
| Child had prenatal substance exposure | 2.411 | 0.71 | .136 | 3.386 | .001 |
| Parent was fully prepared for adoption | −2.252 | 0.71 | −.133 | −3.185 | .002 |
| Child is female | −1.460 | 0.65 | −.087 | −2.255 | .025 |
| Parent completed college | −1.448 | 0.70 | −.082 | −2.082 | .038 |

Note. $F = 26.426$; $p < .0001$; $R^2 = .304$; Adjusted $R^2 = .29$.

## Analysis Using Combined Child and Parent Factors

The researchers performed a final regression analysis combining the six child factors and four parent factors that were significant predictors in the first two analyses. This analysis was to determine how much additional variance the parent factors explained beyond that due to the child factors alone. Of the 10 predictors, 8 loaded in the final regression equation, to account for 30% of the variance. This means that the inclusion of parent factors explained an additional 8% over the 22% explained by child factors alone. Table 4.3 reports the final regression equation.

This final model is able to predict as much as a 22.4-point span in children's BPI scores. The highest scores predicted by this model would involve a male child in a white family, with the parents having less than a college education. This child experienced both prenatal substance exposure and sexual abuse and has significant difficulty giving and receiving affection. The adoptive parents did not believe that they had been fully prepared for adoption, and they needed services for parenting this child that their subsidy did not include. His score would be 24.1.

The best outcome predicted by this model would involve a female child in a minority family, with parents who have college educations. This child did not experience prenatal substance exposure or sexual abuse. She is able to give and receive affection. The parents were fully prepared for adoption and did not need any services that their subsidy did not include. Her score would be 5.3.

These findings provide important guidelines for assessing a child's level of risk for higher levels of behavior problems. Additional research in this area is needed to further develop an understanding of the factors that lead to adjustment difficulties and the interventions that best address these dimensions among adopted children and their families.

# CHAPTER FIVE

# Parents' Comments and Recommendations

Parents had the opportunity to make comments and recommendations on the open-ended questions included throughout the survey. Because so many of the questions focused on needs or problems, the beginning of the survey included a question focusing on strengths. It asked parents to report the best things about their child. Most (81%) did so. The researchers classified the comments as describing the child's ability to relate to others, the child's talents or attributes, or the child's efforts. Many answers included all three types.

By far, the most common responses reflected the child's abilities to relate to others. In more than 70% of responses, parents extolled their children's loving natures, sweetness, kindness to others, compassion, and empathy. They also praised children for talents including intelligence and success in school, musical ability, athleticism, and creativity. Some children were not successful in school, had problems making friends, or were still struggling in their adoptive homes, but parents praised such children for their perseverance and effort.

Although the question asked parents to describe the best things about their children, several responses mixed complaints with praise. For example, one comment read, "She's a loveable child sometimes. She's very, very active. Pretty smart in school." Another wrote, "She is funny and compassionate. Even though she was pretty hyper, her younger years were fun. Her teenage years are a nightmare—I can't wait 'til it's over." A very small number of parents were unable to say anything positive about their children. As one parent wrote, "That's a hard question right now." Another commented that nothing is good about her child.

In addition, several sections asked parents open-ended questions that identified services they thought would help their family. The significant majority of parents offered comments on these sections, although not always identifying particular services. Some took the opportunity to note they were managing well. Some parents identified family strategies or community resources that enabled them to address challenges. The overall themes of their comments have been synthesized in this section.

Several parents used the blank space to tell us how they were faring. Some just wanted to report that they and their children were doing well:

> I don't feel we need any of the above-listed services right now. Things went up and down sometimes, but we made it through.

> When there is a need, we have a family meeting. Everyone has their own opinion and gets to be heard.

> I am not concerned about my child getting along at home or any place, because he is a very well-adjusted child.

The most commonly reported need was for counseling. A number of responses clustered under this category, including the need for specialized counseling, such as expertise with drug-exposed children, specialized assessment, and group therapy. Many parents reported their children were already receiving counseling, and many had been receiving services for several years.

The most common type of response in relation to counseling services had to do with getting care for their children's emotional needs. Parents expressed concern about finding doctors or counselors who accepted the Medicaid card, getting help close to home, and having a choice of providers. Some sought highly specialized help, such as expert help related to attachment problems or PTSD. Additional responses related to the need for respite and residential care, help making children go to counseling, and support groups for children and parents.

A troubling set of comments (tied for second in terms of frequency) addressed parental feelings of hopelessness and inadequacy. The tone of these comments was that parents had tried many types of help to no avail:

What would it take to make things better? A miracle!

I don't know [what would help]. I'm reaching out for help any way I can get it to help this child.

Nothing. He's been like this for 10 years.

We have done it all. Nothing has helped.

Where do I go for help? Can I talk to other parents? I could go on and on. I love, support, and adore this child. How do I help her?

I'm lost.

Parents often identified the need for recreational opportunities as well. Parents desired summer camp, afterschool activities, and special activities for children with physical or mental disabilities or ADHD.

Parents recommended support groups for both parents and children. Parents felt children needed to be in the company of other adopted children who might be struggling with similar issues. They sought parent groups not only for support, but for specific information on raising children with fetal alcohol syndrome, ADHD, and other diagnoses.

Parents with older children wanted services to assist children in moving toward adulthood. As one parent noted, "Our concern is that he will never be independent." Parents suggested vocational training and lifeskills classes, boot camp, and supervised living arrangements.

At the conclusion of the survey, the researchers asked the parents if they had any other recommendations for improving services to adopted children and families. More than 44% of respondents offered suggestions. As elsewhere in the survey, some wrote comments rather than recommendations. Parents also used this opportunity to express their pleasure at having adopted, to praise the services they received, and to offer a word of advice to other adoptive parents. For example, one parent stated,

We have a great family. The first year is for adjusting to each other, letting love grow between parents and child, letting them know how to love and meaning it. As for help for us, it's just time, learning, and understanding each other.

Others wanted to share their success:

Our experience has been wonderful. We had some anxiety at the beginning before adoption assistance was approved, but God wanted us to have this child (we "found" him through circumstances that leave no doubt), and we had faith that He would provide for our child's incredibly high medical costs. No one could have guessed how far this "medically fragile" child has gone. He is an exceptional child!

Our daughter has cerebral palsy. She came to us at 6 years old. She had been in foster care since she was 15 months old. She weighed 24 pounds and wore a size 2T. She had tantrums (bad, self-abusive ones) often. Her shoes...never touched the ground. She had boys' clothes, and her glasses were put together with brown temples and blue frames. She came with absolutely no toys and almost no clothes. Even though she had been in the system for five years! The minute I saw her I loved her and wanted her. Within one year, I had taught her to talk. I remember we were sitting in Osco waiting for a prescription, when she had a complete conversation with a lady there, and the lady actually understood what she said. Of course it was one-word replies to questions like "What's your name?" and "Where do you go to school?" I remember sitting there with tears in my eyes because she was communicating with this lady that had no idea of the milestone we had crossed. She has attended [a] school for handicapped children for five and one-half years. She is talking in complete sentences and even was in a spelling bee last year. Her tantrums had come from her frustration at not being able to communicate. I have had to fight for everything that she has gotten—from doctors, to therapists, to a good school that is able to teach her and understand her disabilities. Now I have this loving, wonderful little girl no one else wanted—who was extremely BD [behavior disorder] and had no social skills—to someone who greets everyone and everyone loves. She is sunshine.

Parents offered many specific recommendations as well. They had no groundswell of demand for extensive services or excessive support. Parents often listed specific needs they felt should be met or asked for services that they had not been able to obtain on their own. Parents' recommendations are shown in Table 5.1.

## Postadoption Support

Parents' recommendations ranged widely in this category. Parents expressed a desire for low-level support such as newsletters, lists of services for adoptive families, and the opportunity to meet with other adoptive parents at conferences, informational sessions, and support groups. Parents felt agencies should follow up in the critical six months to a year after adoption. A commonly expressed need was for someone to call for direction to resources or for information. Several noted that the challenges of parenting children with special needs are not immediately apparent. Support needs to be available as needs arise:

> Mental and emotional problems do not often show up right away. Learning difficulties are not easy to detect....Services need to be available years after adoption for children who do not adjust well. Legal-risk and special-needs children just need more. Parents need help in many ways we can't imagine until it happens.

Parents also sought crisis intervention and in-home counseling when difficulties arose. Some pointed out that early availability of such help might reduce the need for more expensive services later. Parents recommended that services be fully described before finalization, that parents receive an updated list of postadoption services and community supports, and that they know who to call for what assistance. Furthermore, they sought support groups for themselves and their children and intensive, adoption-sensitive services if the need arose.

## Background Information

Parents emphasized the importance of full disclosure of the child's history, as well as that of the child's birth family. Parents spoke poignantly about the impact of knowing too little.

**Table 5.1**
Parents' Recommendations for Services (in percentages)

| | |
|---|---|
| Provide postadoption information, support, and services | 20 |
| Give child and family history/implications of background | 14 |
| Provide additional resources (e.g., child care, recreation) | 12 |
| Improve access/availability of care through Medicaid card | 9 |
| Speed up adoption process | 7 |
| Improve preparation for parents and children | 7 |
| Improve casework and services to family before adoption | 6 |
| Improve availability of competent, skillful providers | 4 |

In cases in which children are prenatally exposed to alcohol and drugs, information should be given to parents that tells you what kind of problems these children might exhibit, along with a list of agencies where certain problems can be diagnosed and counseling the family may need [can be found]. I am so angry that I have spent years going from place to place trying to get diagnosis and services. Families should not have to go through this. It takes away some of the joy that should be part of the adoption process.

Be honest about the child's diagnosis, so the family will know if they are able to take care of a child [with these problems]. We were not told he had fetal alcohol [syndrome], ADHD, was brain injured and mentally delayed. We found this out on our own after the adoption....I feel like they dumped him and ran.

When we adopted, all background information was confidential. We did not know of the mental handicaps of mother and father, all the alcohol abuse of fathers and grandparents, and all the repercussions of neglect and the feelings of worthlessness because adults could not be trusted. We loved and loved, but it made no difference—our house was a battlefield.

In addition to full information, in writing, many parents requested that the implications of their child's background be explained. Even if their child's history was disclosed, they needed to know what that might mean for their child's future. Some argued that all children should have a full psychological evaluation before the placement. Even relative adopters need full information. One parent stated:

> Adoptive parents should be given the history of the birthparents even though they are relatives. My children are the product of my nephew. I have no history regarding their mother. When they ask questions, I cannot give the response they need to hear. Children need to know both birthparents' histories, not just one.

## Resources

Some parental suggestions regarding resources involve expansion of subsidies. These are addressed in the subsidy section. In addition, parents identified educational support and recreational opportunities. Several of the comments dealt with the need for help in getting their children's educational needs met. Recreation for children with special needs was a concern as well. Having access to summer programs, afterschool programs, and community opportunities like Scouts was difficult for children with physical, behavioral, or emotional problems. Parents felt all children needed opportunities to excel, opportunities they could sometimes not afford.

## Speed Up Adoption

A number of parents expressed frustration about the length of time children spent in care prior to adoption. They urged that courts move more quickly and that birthparents be given less time to "get their acts together." As one parent put it:

> The time a child is allowed to remain in foster care when there is no hope of reuniting a birthfamily should have a limit. It isn't fair to the child to be in limbo for years without the legal issues being resolved....A child's life should never be put on hold, not knowing where they'll be next. It's abusive.

Another noted the insensitivity of the court:

> My daughter's birthmother agreed to termination of rights when my daughter was 14 months old, yet this was not done until she was 4 1/2. We had to take her to court and had a meeting in a room with many professionals. In the courtroom, the judge asked someone loudly in front of my child, "Why doesn't the mom want this kid?" This whole experience freaked her out. She was very disturbed for five months or more after this and bit the skin off her hands. She was afraid they would come and take her away.

This is one area in which improvement has already occurred. Given the federal mandates about reducing time in care, parental concerns about children drifting in foster care are likely to diminish.

## Medicaid Card Concerns

Parents echoed the concerns they had raised earlier in the survey about finding doctors and dentists who would accept the Medicaid card. They cited problems of access, distance, and quality of care:

> Medicaid is refused almost everywhere we go. And if it is accepted we are treated differently. Our psychiatrist accepts it and is wonderful. Our counselor does not. Nor does our pediatrician. In addition, insurance has been a nightmare. The minute depression is mentioned, we are refused insurance.

## Subsidy Issues and Additional Services

Although some parents sought higher rates of subsidy, this was not the most common request related to subsidy. Parents felt that the benefits afforded children in foster care should continue after adoption. Several also felt subsidies should be individualized, looking carefully at the needs of a particular child and family.

A few parents requested that subsidy continue through college or through the period when the young adult was making the transition to adulthood. Some parents pointed out that their children were behind developmentally and that additional support was needed to ease them into adult roles and responsibilities.

A related set of recommendations concerned lack of coverage for essential services. Child care, particularly for single parents or for children with serious behavioral or emotional problems, was the service parents identified most commonly as needing additional subsidies. For example:

> [Parents need special help] if the child is a special-needs child such as my son. He has Down's syndrome and profound mental handicap. He is 9 years old, nonverbal, and wears diapers. It is impossible to put him in day care because he is too big to be with the babies but doesn't fit in with the other children. My day care expenses are high because I must hire a private sitter.

Parents also requested tutoring and educational support, transportation, recreational opportunities, and respite. A few parents were struggling with low incomes and sought subsidy increases, better housing, and food stamps. One mother called for providing food stamps to every family.

Very few families specifically mentioned residential care as a needed service. When parents recommended it, however, they saw it as a critically important service.

## Preparation

Parents made both general and specific recommendations about preparation. General advice included requiring training for all parents, not rushing children and families, and forewarning families of the many challenges they may face in adopting a child with a complicated history. Parents urged that families not only be informed of challenges but that they be connected to services they will likely need in the future. Specific suggestions included increasing training related to fetal alcohol syndrome, ADHD, raising multiracial children, and the effects of drug exposure on children beyond early childhood. Respondents also urged that the implications of raising a child with attachment problems should also be emphasized in preparing parents.

## Casework Concerns

A number of parental comments related to inadequate casework. They cited unresponsive caseworkers, constant turnover, withholding information, and inexperience as examples of poor casework:

Caseworkers need to be better informed about the children in their care. Information is inconsistent and contact is infrequent. We found the entire process to be too cumbersome and long. Our child had to be adopted twice due to missed information in the original adoption. To put it bluntly—GET YOUR ACT TOGETHER!!

Six families specifically warned against threatening or forcing parents into adopting. As one parent stated:

Caseworkers should not be telling parents if they do not adopt their relatives, the child will be taken out of your home and never seen again. This puts fear in a family member and they adopt even if they are ill and not prepared to do so.

Although 34 parents expressed significant concerns related to casework, another 21 offered praise. Parents urged the Department of Children and Family Services to keep up the good work and thanked workers for excellent service. As one grandmother stated:

I can't speak for others, but I received all the help before and after I adopted my granddaughter. Whenever I didn't understand something, the [private agency] was there for me. The caseworkers helped me in every way. So I am thanking them again for my granddaughter and for them making this adoption less stressful. THANK YOU!

Others noted:

I would like to thank DCFS for helping me in supporting my adopted daughter. Your support helped more than your department could know. I feel real good about the way my girls have grown. Your department supplied the tools I needed to help them develop. I used the resources wisely. And I believe today me and my family and my adopted daughter share a lifelong bond and I'll always be there for them.

I want to say I've had some of the most wonderful, caring, and knowledgeable people to work with. One caseworker, here at least once a month, sat on the floor and played with my child for a long time. She stated you really have to spend time with them to know more about them and earn their confidence. All the caseworkers I have had bent over backwards to get [birth]parents in compliance.

## Appropriate, Competent Resources

Although some parents spoke to the need for specific services, others wanted existing services to be more helpful to their children. Schools were the most common source of concern. Parents struggled to get their children into appropriate educational settings and to have their children treated with respect. One parent's concerns about school echoed those of several others:

> Our school system is completely insensitive to adopted children including their mental health, ethnic needs, sensitivity, educational needs and occasional downright meanness. [Because my child] takes Prozac, this places a red flag over her head and is discriminatory in the worst way.

In addition, parents expressed their need for counselors who understood their children, who had expertise in areas such as reactive attachment disorder, and who fully included parents in the counseling endeavor.

## Other Concerns and Recommendations

Parents offered a number of other recommendations that could not be neatly classified. Several reported the difficulties of maintaining contact between siblings adopted separately. They saw the importance of such contact but were frustrated with long distances between siblings or, in a few cases, lack of cooperation from other adoptive parents. A few expressed concern about maintaining contact with birthfamily members, believing it to be detrimental to the child. Parents asked for advice about telling children they were adopted and sharing difficult information about the child's past.

Other parents offered words of wisdom or advice to parents and talked about the blessing that the adopted child had been in their lives. All in all, we found it heartening that parents, after completing a lengthy survey, took the time to offer so many comments and recommendations.

# PART II
# A COMPARISON OF KIN, FOSTER, AND
# MATCHED ADOPTIVE FAMILIES

# CHAPTER SIX

# Overview of Kinship Care

In Illinois, as in some other states, much of the marked increase in movement from foster care to adoption is due to systematic efforts to encourage relatives to adopt children in their care. Part II of this volume examines the responses of the 523 relative adoptive parents who returned surveys and compares them to those of 589 foster adoptive parents and 183 parents who were matched with their children.

Much of what researchers know about relative caregivers comes from the fairly recent literature on kin foster care. This literature tells us such care has dramatically increased in recent years. For example, the U.S. Department of Health and Human Services (USDHHS), through its Adoption and Foster Care Analysis and Reporting System (AFCARS) system, reports that in responding states as of September 30, 1997, 32% of children in the child welfare system were in kinship foster care. Illinois has been a leader in placing children with kin (Testa, 1993). In Illinois, California, and Florida, between 46% and 51% of children were in kin foster care homes by the mid 1990s (Testa, 1993; U.S. Children's Bureau, 2000). Kinship care is the fastest growing type of out-of-home placement (Gleeson & Craig, 1994), and researchers expect this trend to increase.

Most people recognize kinship care as having clear benefits for children, including greater placement stability, increased likelihood of being placed with siblings, a closer connection with members of their immediate families, and less maltreatment in out-of-home care (Berrick, Barth, & Needell, 1994; Le Prohn, 1994; Scannapieco, Hegar, & McAlpine, 1997). Furthermore, many child welfare experts have a philosophical preference for kin care and believe that children are better served when cared for by family members within their communities of origin (Chipungu, 1991; CWLA, 1994; Hegar, 1999).

At the same time, kin care has drawbacks. Children placed with kin are less likely to be reunified with their birthparents, are likely to be in care longer before reunification does occur, and are less likely to be adopted than other children (Barth, Courtney, Berrick, & Albert, 1994; Berrick et al., 1994; Wulczyn & Goerge, 1992). Kin-placed children also are less likely to receive needed mental health and medical services (Dubowitz, Feigelman, & Zuravin, 1993). Furthermore, researchers have lingering concerns about the ability of relatives, particularly grandparents, to set appropriate boundaries with birthparents and to adequately protect children. This concern is exacerbated by evidence that kin care providers receive much less monitoring and support than other foster care providers, as well as by their having lower income and more children (Berrick et al., 1994; Dubowitz et al., 1993; National Commission on Foster Care, 1991). Despite such concerns, the preference for children to be placed with relatives when in out-of-home care is now federal policy (Berrick & Barth, 1994; Dubowitz et al., 1993).

Studies of kinship foster care reveal that most kinship care is female kin care, with grandmothers providing care in the majority of cases, and aunts comprising the second-largest category of caregivers (Dubowitz et al., 1993; Scannapieco et al., 1997; Task Force on Permanency Planning for Foster Children, 1990). Kin care providers are more likely to be single parents than nonrelative caregivers, and they are likely to be older than other foster parents (Berrick et al., 1994; Dubowitz et al., 1993; Le Prohn, 1994; Scannapieco et al., 1997). Studies of kinship care arrangements reveal that children placed with kin are predominantly African American (Dubowitz et al., 1993; Leslie, Lansverk, Horton, Ganger, & Newton, 2000; Scannapieco & Jackson, 1996). Also, relative caregivers typically have less education than nonrelative foster parents (Berrick et al., 1994; Le Prohn, 1994).

Kin caregivers typically feel strong commitment to the children for whom they care (Berrick et al., 1994; Dubowitz et al., 1993). They are more committed to facilitating the child's relationship with birthfamily members than with nonrelative caregivers (Le Prohn, 1994). In a study of Baltimore children in care, Dubowitz and his colleagues (1993) found that only 9% of relative foster parents described the children as difficult to care for. Those children who were older, however, were more difficult than younger children. Older children had more mental health problems, including acting-out behavior.

Some authors argue that kinship care has been described too broadly and that it is important to consider the variations within kinship care. Leslie and her colleagues (2000) examined the situations of 484 children in a county in California who had some kin placement experience. They identified three subgroups of children: (1) children placed in kinship care, with no placements in other foster care or more restrictive settings; (2) children with placement experience with both kin and traditional foster care; and (3) children placed with kin who also had experience in a more restrictive setting, such as a group home or treatment center. Most children in the study (72%) spent time both in kin and family foster care, but 19% were placed with kin only (Leslie et al., 2000).

Leslie et al. (2000) found that children who were or had been placed with kin had very different experiences when compared by subgroup. Those placed only with kin tended to be young and were in care primarily due to neglect. Those with both kin and foster care experience were even younger and had experienced a wider range of maltreatment. Children who had been in more restrictive settings as well as kin care were older and had experienced more maltreatment and multiple types of maltreatment.

There were important ethnic differences in this study. African American children were more likely to have kin-only experience than any other type. Hispanic children were much more likely to have been placed in both traditional homes and kin foster homes than to have kin-only or restrictive setting care. Fully 80% of Hispanic children had both types of care. Asian children were overrepresented among children experiencing care in restrictive settings. Leslie and her colleagues (2000) concluded that "the concept of kinship care is complex and not well captured by a dichotomous variable" (p. 331).

## Kinship Adoption

Child welfare scholars have begun to study kinship foster care and assess its value as a placement option for children, although much remains to be known. Less is known about kinship adoption.

Magruder (1994) compared relative and nonrelative adoptive parents of children placed from the child welfare system. He found that relative adopters were more likely to be single parents, be older, and have less formal education and lower incomes than nonrelative adopters. Children adopted by relatives had spent slightly more time in the foster care system, but had spent more of that time in the home of their adoptive parents.

Children adopted by kin were more than twice as likely to be adopted by a single parent, almost all of whom were female. Relative adopters were slightly older than nonrelative adopters, on average, but there was also more variation in age among relatives. Education and income levels were much higher for nonrelatives. This was particularly true for relatives adopting Hispanic and African American children. Magruder found that the median earned family income for white relative adopters was 76% of that of adopting nonrelatives. The median income for the families of Hispanic and African American children adopted by a relative was much lower. Hispanic relative adopters earned only 49% of what nonrelative adopters did, and African American relative adopters earned just 42% of nonrelatives. Thus, children adopted by relatives were likely to have considerably lower household incomes than children adopted by others. Much of this difference can be explained by the lower educational levels of relative adopters, their somewhat higher ages, and the fact that so many are single parents.

Rosenthal and Groze (1992), in their longitudinal study of the outcomes of special needs adoption, found that kin adoptions received some of the most favorable assessments. Kin adoptions were more likely than other adoption types to be rated as having very positive outcomes. This was particularly the case for grandparent adopters, in which 73% of respondents rated them as very positive. Respondents assessed 48% of relative adoptions by aunts, uncles, or cousins, and 29% of adoptions by other relatives, as very positive.

Barth (1993), examined the outcomes of 320 adopted children identified as prenatally drug-exposed compared with 456 non–drug exposed children and 620 children whose drug exposure history was unknown. He found that relatives represented about 10% of all adoptions, and relatives were more likely to adopt children who had been drug-exposed than nonrelative adopters were.

These limited studies suggest that relatives are willing to adopt children from the child welfare system. Although children placed with relatives are likely to grow up in a single parent family with limited income, adoptions by kin may have more positive outcomes than other adoption types.

## The Illinois Experience

Illinois has been a leader in moving children to permanency through adoption, and this is often achieved by kin adoption. As seen in Table 6.1, adoptions by relatives have eclipsed foster parent adoptions, and at the time of this study, kin adoptions accounted for the largest number of adoptions of children in state care in Illinois.

By 1998, 50% of adoptions were by relatives, and by 1999, 57%. Most other states have not yet moved to relative adoption to such a degree. For the 46,000 children adopted through the public child welfare system in federal FY 1999, only 15% were adopted by kin (U.S. Children's Bureau, 2000).

## Differences in Adoptive Families by Type

Illinois's practice of placing children with family when feasible is reflected in the surveys received. Among families returning surveys, 39% (523) were formed through adoption by relatives. Of responses, 44% (589) came from foster parent adopters, and 14% (183) from those who were matched with the child for the purpose of adoption. Another 2.8% were listed as "other." These were typically adoptive parents who had known the child previously, for example, parents who adopted a child who had been the foster child of a friend.

Differences existed across several demographic variables by adoption type. Relative adopters were much more likely to be members of minority racial or ethnic groups ($\chi^2$ = 268.13, $p < .001$). Of kin adopters, 82% of relative adopters were nonwhite—77% were African American, 4% were Hispanic, and 1% were Native American. Only 18% were white. The majority of both foster and matched adoptive parents were white—62% and 73%, respectively. Among foster parent adopters, 35% were African American and 3% were Hispanic. For matched families, 26% were African American, 2% were Native American, and 2% were Hispanic.

**Table 6.1**
Child Welfare Adoptions by Year and Type

| Fiscal Year | Relative | Foster | Matched | Total |
|---|---|---|---|---|
| 1995 | 680 | 759 | 201 | 1,640 |
| 1996 | 875 | 825 | 261 | 1,961 |
| 1997[a] | 737 | 868 | 160 | 2,229 |
| 1998 | 2,139 | 1,869 | 285 | 4,293 |
| 1999 | 4,179 | 2,954 | 182 | 7,315 |
| Total | 8,610 | 7,275 | 829 | 17,438 |

[a]Data for 11 months, with one region not reporting by type. Data adapted from the Illinois Department of Children and Family Services data department.

Relatives also were much more likely to be single parents ($\chi^2 = 190.21$, $p < .001$). This was true of 60% of relative homes, compared with only 29% of foster adoptive and 21% of matched homes ($\chi^2 = 164.99$, $p < .001$). Relatives also have less education than foster or matched adoptive parents, as shown in Table 6.2.

Thus, 43% of responding relative adopters had a high school education or less, compared to 24% of foster and 9% of matched parents. This lower educational attainment, and the high percentage of single-parent families among relative adopters, contribute to differences in income. The survey asked respondents to report their incomes exclusive of adoption subsidy. As indicated in Figure 6.1, relative adopters had much lower incomes than either of the other types ($\chi^2 = 275.11$, $p < .001$).

The fact that 62% of relative adoptive families reported incomes of less than $25,000 per year, and 79% have incomes less than $35,000, underscores the importance of financial subsidies to relative adopters. Many foster families also had low incomes, although far fewer than relative adopters. Nearly one-third (31%) of foster families had incomes of less than $25,000, exclusive of subsidy.

Relatives were more likely to adopt sibling groups ($\chi^2 = 59.38$, $p < .001$). Of relatives, 58% reported adopting siblings, compared with 42% of foster parent and 28% of matched adopters.

**Table 6.2**

Education Level of Parent by Type of Adoption (in percentages)

| Educational Level[a] | Relative | Foster | Matched |
|---|---|---|---|
| Less than high school completion | 25 | 9 | 3 |
| Completed high school | 18 | 16 | 6 |
| Some post–high school education | 43 | 43 | 39 |
| College degree and beyond | 15 | 33 | 52 |

[a] Data refer to parent with highest educational level.

Relative adopters and foster parent adopters were older, on average, than matched adopters ($F = 83.25$, $p < .001$). The mean age of relative adoptive mothers was 52, compared with 49 and 46 for foster and matched adoptive parents, respectively ($F = 83.245$, $p < .001$). The significant majority of matched parents (75%) were younger than 50, compared with 43% of relative and 56% of foster parents. This age differential continued across age groups. For example, 27% of relative adoptive parents were 60 or older, compared with 14% of foster parents and just 5% of matched parents. Age groups by type of adoption are presented in Table 6.3.

The basic demographic data on relative adoptions in this study mirrors that of Magruder's (1994) study of kin adoption, as well as several studies on kinship foster care. Relative adoptive parents are somewhat older, have less education, and have much less family income than other adopters. They are more likely to be single parents and to adopt sibling groups. The majority—more than 8 in 10—of relative adopters are racial or ethnic minorities, with 3 of 4 being African American. The majority of both foster and matched adopters are white.

The survey did not ask the nature of the preadoptive relationship among kin adopters. To the extent that kin adoption in Illinois mirrors kin foster care placement, it is likely that most adopters are grandmothers or aunts of the children they adopt.

**Figure 6.1**
Family Yearly Income by Type of Adoption (in percentages)

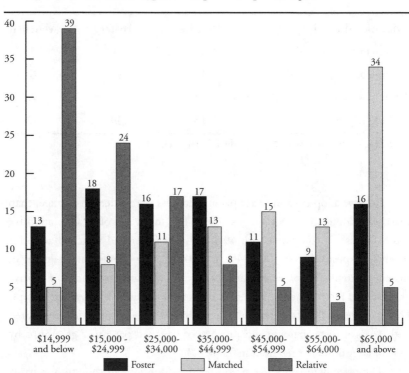

## Differences in Child Characteristics by Adoption Type

When researchers examined adoptions by type, differences in child characteristics became clear. Considerable differences existed by race and ethnicity. Children adopted by relatives were much more likely to be African American—76% of relative-adopted children were African American, compared with 48% of those adopted by foster parents and 38% of those adopted by matched parents ($\chi^2 = 109.94$, $p < .001$).

Children adopted by relatives and foster parents were somewhat younger at the time of survey completion than children in matched adoptive homes ($F = 228.42$, $p < .001$). The overall mean age was 12.0 years. Children adopted by relatives had a mean age of 11.9, compared with 12.0 for those adopted by foster parents and 13.0 for those in matched adoptions.

**Table 6.3**
Current Maternal Age Category by Family Type (in percentages)

| Age Range | Relative | Foster | Matched |
|---|---|---|---|
| 20–29 | 2 | 1 | 0 |
| 30–39 | 13 | 15 | 17 |
| 40–49 | 28 | 41 | 57 |
| 50–59 | 30 | 29 | 21 |
| 60–69 | 20 | 11 | 5 |
| 70 and older | 7 | 3 | 0 |

No statistically significant difference existed in age at placement with this family. Of all respondents, 70% of relative children and 78% of foster children were 5 or younger when placed in their current homes, as were 72% of matched children. Children placed with relatives, however, were older when they first entered the child welfare system—3.2 years for relatives, 2.2 for foster parent adopters, and 1.8 for matched adopters ($F = 369.87$, $p < .001$).

Although children were similar in age at the time of placement in what became their adoptive family, they had differences in their paths to those homes. Children placed with relatives were placed in their eventual adoptive homes much sooner than children in other homes ($F = 210.81$, $p < .001$). On average, children adopted by relatives spent 9.8 months in the child welfare system before being placed with them. By comparison, children adopted by foster parents spent an average of 1.1 years from first removal until placement in what became their adoptive homes. Children in matched adoptive homes were in the system 2.1 years on average prior to adoptive placement.

Despite being placed more quickly into what became their adoptive homes, children adopted by relatives waited much longer before becoming adopted, an average of 4.0 years. Foster adoptive children waited nearly as long—3.5 years from the time they were placed in the home where they were adopted until finalization ($F = 1046.75$, $p < .001$). Matched children achieved adoption much more quickly once placed in their adoptive homes, an average of 1.1 years. Because matched homes are, by definition, preadoptive homes, it is not surprising that these children wait shorter periods of time to achieve adoption.

**Table 6.4**
Adverse Factors by Adoption Type (in percentages)

| Factor | Relative | Foster | Matched |
|---|---|---|---|
| Had physical abuse history*** | 23 | 40 | 35 |
| Had sexual abuse history*** | 12 | 19 | 20 |
| Experienced serious neglect*** | 59 | 69 | 56 |
| Had two or more foster homes prior*** | 18 | 45 | 50 |
| Had psychiatric/ residential placement prior | 8 | 11 | 9 |
| Had previous adoptive placement** | 11 | 13 | 23 |
| Moved back and forth between birthfamily and foster care | 16 | 19 | 22 |
| Exposed to alcohol/ drugs prenatally*** | 59 | 63 | 51 |

$**p < .01.$ $***p < .001.$

Although workers placed children adopted by relatives with their eventual adopters more quickly than other children, the children adopted by kin spent the most time in the system before achieving legal permanency. Overall, children averaged 4.5 years from the time they were first removed from their birthfamily to adoption finalization. Children adopted by relatives waited the longest from first removal to adoption finalization (4.8 years), but children adopted by foster parents waited almost as long (4.6 years). Those adopted in matched homes spent the least time between removal and adoption, but still averaged 3.4 years ($F = 242.93$, $p < .001$).

In summary, children adopted by relatives are much more likely than other children to be African American, and these children spend less time in the child welfare system before being placed in adoptive homes. Both children adopted by relatives and foster parents waited longer to become adopted from their point of entry into the child welfare system than children in matched homes. Children in matched homes, however, spent much longer in the system before ending up in what became their permanent home.

**Table 6.5**
Children's Special Needs (in percentages)

| Special Need | Relative | Foster | Matched |
| --- | --- | --- | --- |
| Vision or hearing impairment | 26 | 35 | 45 |
| Physical handicap | 2 | 8 | 15 |
| Mental retardation | 3 | 10 | 17 |
| Chronic medical problems | 11 | 21 | 24 |
| Learning disability | 37 | 54 | 57 |
| Emotional disturbance | 24 | 42 | 46 |
| Behavior problem | 43 | 57 | 55 |
| Developmental delay | 17 | 39 | 51 |

Note. $p < .001$ for each chi-square.

## Children's Backgrounds

Children come to adoption with a variety of experiences that can complicate their adjustment. The survey asked parents to identify adverse conditions or experiences in their child's history. As Table 6.4 indicates, children adopted by relatives had fewer adverse factors than children adopted in other types of homes $(F = 187.97, p < .001)$. These children averaged 1.7 adverse factors, compared with 2.4 for children adopted by foster parents. Children adopted in matched families averaged 2.3.

Children adopted by relatives had fewer prior adverse experiences than children in foster or matched homes, with the exception of serious neglect and prenatal substance exposure. Relatives also were more likely to report they knew important aspects of the child's history, particularly the child's maltreatment history. For example, the highest unsure response among relative adopters was for whether the child had been sexually abused prior to the placement (15%). For foster parent and matched adopters, uncertainty about sexual abuse was much more common—32% of foster parents and 28% of matched adopters. Prenatal drug exposure was another area in which relatives were far more likely to report they knew the child's history. Only 10% reported they were uncertain, whereas 27% of foster parents and 32% of matched parents did not know if their child had been prenatally exposed to alcohol or drugs.

Parents also reported on the presence and severity of disabilities, conditions, or problems affecting their child. As shown in Table 6.5, relative adopters were much less likely to report that their child had disabilities or other problems or that such problems were severe when present. Foster and matched parents' reports were more similar, although matched parents reported the highest level of special needs overall.

## Preparation and Subsidy

Those responding to the survey provided information on their preparation for adoption and the services they received after adoptive placement. As a group, kin adopters were least likely to receive training prior to the adoption. When parents did receive training, however, relatives reported receiving more hours of training than foster parent adopters (a mean of 14.5). Foster parents reported an average of 12.3 hours, and matched parents, 15.3. Relative adopters were the most positive of the groups about the benefits of training (see Table 6.6).

The survey asked parents how well they were prepared by the professionals assisting them in adoption. Relative adopters believed that they and their children were fully prepared in 75% of cases, and very few believed they and their children were poorly prepared. Foster parents were less positive than relative adopters, but were still positive. Of foster parent adopters, 51% reported feeling fully prepared, and 60% reported that their children were fully prepared. Of foster adopters, however, 12% said they were poorly prepared. Once again, matched adopters were the least positive—40% stated they had been fully prepared, and 31% said this was the case for their child. In the matched group, 9% of parents and 15% of children were rated by parents as poorly prepared ($\chi^2 = 1\,05.88$, $p < .001$).

Relatives believed preparation could have been better in only 20% of cases. This was true for 34% of foster adoptive parents, and 42% of matched adoption ($\chi^2 = 44.42$, $p < .001$). The most commonly cited lack, in all types of cases, was the need for full disclosure or information about the child's background.

To be included in the study, families had to be receiving an adoption subsidy. The survey asked parents to list the additional components of their subsidy, beyond financial support. Children adopted by relatives were less likely to receive additional subsidies related to counseling, but were more likely to receive additional help related to medical care.

**Table 6.6**
Training Participation and Rating of Helpfulness

| Type | Percentage Receiving | Very Helpful | Somewhat Helpful | Not at All Helpful |
|---|---|---|---|---|
| Relative | 42 | 71 | 28 | 2 |
| Foster | 49 | 43 | 51 | 6 |
| Matched | 66 | 40 | 57 | 3 |

Note. $\chi^2$ = 51.109; $p < .001$.

# References

Barth, R. P. (1993). Revisiting the issues: Adoption of drug-exposed children. *Adoption, 3,* 167–175.

Barth, R. P., Courtney, M. E., Berrick, J. D., & Albert, V. (1994). *From child abuse to permanency planning: Child welfare services, pathways and placements.* Hawthorne, NY: Aldine.

Berrick, J. D., & Barth, R. P. (1994). Research on kinship foster care: What do we know? Where do we go from here? *Children & Youth Services Review, 16,* 1–5.

Berrick, J. D., Barth, R. P., & Needell, B. (1994). A comparison of kinship homes and foster family homes: Implications for kinship care as family preservation. *Children & Youth Services Review, 16,* 33–63.

Child Welfare League of America. (1994). *Kinship care: A natural bridge.* Washington, DC: Author.

Chipungu, S. (1991). A value-based policy framework. In J. E. Everett, S. S. Chipungu, & B. R. Leashore (Eds.), *Child welfare: An Africentric perspective* (pp. 290–305). New Brunswick, NJ: Rutgers University Press.

Dubowitz, H., Feigelman, S., & Zuravin, S. (1993). A profile of kinship care. *Child Welfare, 72,* 153–169.

Gleeson, J. P., & Craig, L. C. (1994). Kinship care in child welfare: An analysis of states' policies. *Children & Youth Services Review, 16,* 7–31.

Hegar, R. (1999). The cultural roots of kinship care. In R. Hegar & M. Scannapieco (Eds.), *Kinship foster care: Policy, research, and practice.* New York: Oxford University Press.

Le Prohn, N. (1994) The role of the kinship foster parent: A comparison of role conceptions of relative and non-relative foster parents. *Children & Youth Services Review, 16,* 65–84.

Leslie, L. K., Lansverk, J., Horton, M. B., Ganger, W., & Newton, R. R. (2000). The heterogeneity of children and their experiences in kinship care. *Child Welfare, 79,* 315–334.

Magruder, J. (1994). Characteristics of relative and non-relative adoptions by California public adoption agencies. *Children & Youth Services Review, 16,* 123–131.

National Commission on Foster Care. (1991). *A blueprint for fostering infants, children and youths in the 1990s.* Washington, DC: Child Welfare League of America.

Rosenthal, J. A., & Groze, V. K. (1992). *Special-needs adoption: A study of intact families.* Westport, CT: Praeger.

Scannapieco, M., Hegar, R. L., & McAlpine, C. (1997). Kinship care and foster care: A comparison of characteristics and outcomes. *Families and Society, 78,* 480–488.

Scannapieco, M., & Jackson, S. (1996). Kinship care: The African-American resilient response to family preservation. Social Work, 41, 190–196.

Task Force on Permanency Planning for Foster Children. (1990). *Kinship foster care: The double-edged dilemma.* Rochester, NY: Author.

Testa, M. (1993). *Home of relative (HMR) reform in Illinois. Interim report.* Chicago: School of Social Service Administration, University of Chicago.

U.S. Children's Bureau. (2000). *Statistics on special needs adoption.* Available from http://www.acf.dhhs.gov/programs/cb/.

Wulczyn, F., & Goerge, R. (1992). *Public policy and the dynamics of foster care: A multi-state study of placement histories. Research Report to the U.S. Department of Health and Human Services.* Chicago: Chapin Hall Center for Children.

# CHAPTER SEVEN

# Children's Level of Adjustment in Kinship, Foster, and Matched Adoptions

Children generally fare well after adoption, according to their parents. When research compares children by type of adoption, however, important differences emerge. In this chapter, the researchers analyzed the adjustments of children after adoption by type of adoption. Although subsets of children and families were struggling in each group, it was parents whose children had been matched for adoption who reported the highest level of need. Ratings of children adopted by foster parents came close to those of matched children on many items, however.

## At Home

On questions about overall functioning of the child, relative adopters generally gave the most positive responses, followed by foster parents. The matched adoptive parents reported the highest level of problems throughout the survey on most items. On some questions, the differences were small. On other questions, however, responses were quite different. For example, in relation to children's overall functioning at home, 91% of relative adopters rated children as excellent or good, as compared with 88% of foster and 83% of matched adopters. Differences were greater on the question about whether a child's special needs made it difficult to find child care—only 12% of relatives responded "very difficult," compared with 26% of matched and 22% of foster adopters ($\chi^2$ = 14.14, $p < .05$).

In relation to children's abilities compared with others of the same age, relative adopters rated children as more capable. Table 7.1 shows a few com-

**Table 7.1**
Satisfactory Ratings on Children's Abilities (in percentages)

| Ability | Relative | Foster | Matched |
| --- | --- | --- | --- |
| Follow instructions | 85 | 73 | 71 |
| Make good decisions | 80 | 65 | 60 |
| Handle anger/frustration | 71 | 56 | 56 |

Note. All chi-square tests significant at $p < .001$.

parisons of the percentage of children rated fairly well or very well on specific abilities in which differences were greatest.

Attachment-related problems were less common in relative adoptive families. Only 8% of relative adopters rated their children as "poor" or "not at all" on their ability to give and receive affection. For children of foster adoptive parents, the rate was 13%, and for matched parents, 16% ($\chi^2 = 19.05$, $p < .01$).

Also, relative adopters reported feeling closer to their children than other types of adoptive parents did—90% responded "very close" on this question, compared with 73% of matched and 80% of foster adoptive parents. Ratings of "not at all close" were very rare (only 2% overall). Of matched adoptive parents, however, 5% reported they were not at all close to their child, compared with only 0.6% of relative adopters ($\chi^2 = 37.87$, $p < .001$).

Judging an adopted child as having a negative effect on the family also was less common in relative adoptive families ($\chi^2 = 27.98$, $p < .001$). Whereas 9% of matched adoptive parents reported the child had a negative or very negative effect, only 1.4% of relative adopters reported negative effects. The rate was 4.5% in foster adoptive families.

Likewise, reporting that the adoption had weakened their relationship with a spouse or partner was most common in matched adoptive families (19%), compared with 9% of relative adoptions. The rate was 15% for foster adoptive families ($\chi^2 = 14.99$, $p < .01$).

## At School

Overall, relative adopters reported fewer school problems than other types of adoptive families on almost all measures. In relation to the child's overall adjustment in school, 26% of relatives rated their children as fair or poor, compared with 34% of foster and 38% of matched adoptive parents ($\chi^2$ = 11.01, $p < .01$). Children of relative adopters had a higher rate of suspensions (30%), however, than the 21% of children of foster and 24% of matched adopters ($\chi^2$ = 11.01, $p < .01$).

Several measures on school adjustment are included in Table 7.2. Children in relative adoptive families were less likely to receive special education services for learning problems than children in other kinds of adoptive families. Also, the relative adopters' children were much less likely to be on medication for ADHD or other behavioral problems. Their incidence of some other school problems was close to that of foster adoptive families, but significantly less than matched adoptive families, such as the percentage repeating a grade.

The same number of relative adoptive parents reported that their children had unmet educational needs, however, as other types of adoptive parents did. In choosing services they thought would help, relative adoptive parents were more likely than others to request afterschool programs for children.

## Children's Physical and Mental Health

Differences in children's physical and mental health emerged when the researchers examined adoptions by type. Overall, 8% of children were reported to be in less than good physical health in all types of adoptive families, and 29% of parents reported their children have special medical needs. Children in relative adoptive homes, however, were less likely to have special medical needs (19%) than those in foster (33%) or matched (40%) adoptive families ($\chi^2$ = 36.96, $p < .001$).

As expected given their lower incomes, a higher percentage of relative adopters (79%) depended on Medicaid for all or almost all of the costs of their children's medical care than other types of adoptive homes. Of other types of homes, 63 % of foster adoptive parents and 45% of matched parents report-

**Table 7.2**
Indicators of School Adjustment (in percentages)

| Variable | Relative | Foster | Matched |
|---|---|---|---|
| Special education/ language problems*** | 29 | 46 | 53 |
| Medication for behaviors*** | 16 | 39 | 46 |
| Repeating a grade** | 24 | 24 | 35 |
| Teacher complaints regarding behavior* | 50 | 54 | 61 |
| Grades mostly Ds and Fs* | 14 | 18 | 23 |

*$p < .05$. **$p < .01$. ***$p < .001$.

ed they relied on Medicaid for all or most of the costs of medical care ($\chi^2$ = 86.7, $p < .001$). Yet relative adoptive parents had the lowest incidence of complaints about experiencing difficulty getting adequate medical services for their children ($\chi^2$ = 11.66, $p < .01$). Of relative parents, 10% (compared with 16% of foster adoptive parents and 19% of matched parents) reported difficulty.

Children's behavior and emotional problems were markedly different by type of adoption. Relative adopters reported concerns about children's mental health and behavior much less commonly. Of them, 18% rated their children as experiencing fair to poor mental health, compared with 29% of foster adoptive parents and 34% of matched parents ($\chi^2$ = 50.58, $p < .001$). In addition, only 2% of related children had been placed in residential treatment since adoption, compared with 7% of foster adopted children and 11% of matched children ($\chi^2$ = 19.21, $p < .001$). This is of particular interest in light of the fact that children placed with relatives are more similar to others in relation to having psychiatric or residential placement prior to adoption. These rates of residential placement, as shown earlier in Table 6.4, were 8% for children adopted by kin, 11% for foster adopted children, and 9% for matched children.

**Table 7.3**
Behavior Problem Index (BPI) Score by Adoptive Family Type

| Family Type | BPI Score |
|-------------|-----------|
| Relative | 9.76 |
| Foster | 13.12 |
| Matched | 13.12 |

Children living with relatives had lower behavior problem scores ($\chi^2$ = 122.02, $p$ < .001). The mean BPI score for children in each type of adoptive family is listed in Table 7.3.

This is not to say that children in relative adoptive families do not have significant problems, only that fewer of them have significant problems. For example, the percentage of children with BPI scores of 15 or above, a point at which children are likely receiving psychological help (Zill, 1994), is 27% for children adopted by relatives, 47% for foster adopted children, and 45% for matched adoptive families ($\chi^2$ = 38.67, $p$ < .001).

## Adjustment in Neighborhood and Community

Fewer relative adoptive parents (13%) reported concerns about their children getting along in their neighborhood and community than other types of adoptive parents (26% for foster, 37% for matched). Table 7.4 reports the percentages of children rated "fairly well" or "very well" on these abilities to function in their community. The level of problems is clearly greatest among matched adoptive families and lowest among relative adoptive families ($\chi^2$ = 54.41, $p$ < .001).

In summary, on measures of children's functioning at home and in the community, relative adopters reported much higher functioning. Rates of school concerns for children adopted by relatives were similar to children adopted by foster or matched parents, however. Although school was reported to be more problematic for relative adopted children than other aspects of their lives, they still fared better in school on most reported items.

**Table 7.4**
Satisfactory Ratings of Children's Abilities to Function in their
Community (in percentages)

| Ability | Relative | Foster | Matched |
|---|---|---|---|
| Make friends with children of similar age | 93 | 78 | 69 |
| Get along with children in neighborhood | 93 | 87 | 81 |
| Choose friends parent is comfortable with | 86 | 81 | 72 |
| Make good decisions | 83 | 68 | 59 |
| Fit in with organized groups | 90 | 78 | 67 |

Note. Chi-square tests significant at $p < .001$ on all items.

## Attitudes About Adoption

The survey used several variables to capture the overall adoption experience of these families. It asked parents to rate how difficult the child had been to raise, how close they felt to the child, their degree of satisfaction with their adoption experience, and whether they would adopt this child again, knowing what they now know. The good news is that parents in all categories generally responded positively about their children. On every question, however, relatives responded more positively than foster or matched adoptive parents.

Whereas 25% of relative parents reported their children were moderately to very difficult to raise, 48% of foster parents and 52% of matched parents did so (see Table 7.5). Furthermore, relatives rarely rated children as very difficult to raise. Foster adoptive parents were more than twice as likely to rate their children as very difficult, and matched parents were three times more likely to do so.

Despite finding a quarter to half of children difficult to raise, almost all parents across types of adoption reported feeling close to their children, as shown in Table 7.6. They also were satisfied with their adoption experience and would adopt their children again, knowing everything they now know (see Tables 7.7 and 7.8). Although all types of parents were quite positive in these responses, relative parents again were the most positive. Although dis-

**Table 7.5**
How Difficult Is Child to Raise? (in percentages)

| Rating | Relative | Foster | Matched |
|---|---|---|---|
| Not at all difficult | 38 | 22 | 22 |
| A little difficult | 37 | 29 | 27 |
| Moderately difficult | 19 | 33 | 31 |
| Very difficult | 6 | 15 | 21 |

Note. $\chi^2$ = 87.05; $p < .001$.

**Table 7.6**
Closeness to Child (in percentages)

| Rating | Relative | Foster | Matched |
|---|---|---|---|
| Very | 90 | 80 | 73 |
| Somewhat | 10 | 17 | 23 |
| Not at all | 0.6 | 2 | 5 |

Note. $\chi^2$ = 37.87; $p < .001$.

satisfaction was rare overall, more than twice as many foster parents and three times as many matched adoptive parents were dissatisfied as relative adopters.

Asking a parent, "Knowing everything you now know, if you had it to do over again would you adopt this child?" is provocative. Stating that one would not adopt a child again, if given a second opportunity, requires a parent to admit a hard truth. In each adoption type, the significant majority of parents reported they would definitely adopt their children again. Very few parents stated they definitely would not adopt. Of those parents who said they probably would not adopt their child again, however, matched parents were more than twice as likely as relative adopters to state they probably would not adopt (see Table 7.8).

**Table 7.7**

Satisfaction with Adoption Experience (in percentages)

| Rating | Relative | Foster | Matched |
|---|---|---|---|
| Very satisfied | 66 | 55 | 54 |
| Satisfied | 30 | 35 | 32 |
| Dissatisfied or very dissatisfied | 4 | 10 | 14 |

Note. $\chi^2$ = 28.68; $p$ < .001.

**Table 7.8**

Would Adopt Child Again (in percentages)

| Rating | Relative | Foster | Matched |
|---|---|---|---|
| Yes, definitely | 81 | 74 | 68 |
| Probably | 15 | 18 | 22 |
| Probably would not | 4 | 8 | 10 |
| Definitely would not | 0 | 1 | 0 |

Note. $\chi^2$ = 19.86; $p$ < .01.

Parents also rated their children's feelings about being adopted. Very few parents reported that their children felt negatively about adoption. The percentages that rated children as feeling positive or mixed were very similar for relative and foster adopted children. Matched parents, however, were less likely to report their children felt positively (see Table 7.9).

Although the majority of parents in all adoption types were positive about adoption, across the board, relative adopters were more positive in their ratings about their children and about the adoption experience, and matched adopters were less positive.

**Table 7.9**
Child's Feelings About Adoption (in percentages)

| Rating | Relative | Foster | Matched |
|---|---|---|---|
| Positive | 76 | 71 | 61 |
| Mixed | 23 | 27 | 35 |
| Negative | 1 | 2 | 4 |

Note. $\chi^2$ = 16.44; $p < .01$.

# Reference

Zill, N. (1994). *Adopted children in the United States: A profile based on a national survey of child health.* Washington, DC: Child Trends.

# CHAPTER EIGHT

# Birthfamily Contact

Adoption practitioners in the United States have given growing support to maintaining contact between adopted children and their birthfamilies. Most of the discussion and the limited study that have occurred have focused on non-special-needs adoptions of infants. Practitioners have directed much less attention to contact between adoptive families and birthfamilies when children come to adoption as a result of maltreatment, although workers have increasing interest in exploring contact in child welfare adoptions as well. As Silverstein and Roszia (1999) noted, "Regardless of the situation of the adoptee or the circumstances of the adoption, the goal of openness is to minimize loss and to maintain connections" (p. 636).

Postadoption contact is usually classified as *open adoption*. This term is far from precise and is used to describe everything from direct, ongoing contact between birthparents and the adoptive family to indirect contact through an intermediary, in which the birthparents and adoptive parents do not have identifying information about one another. Although *open adoption* means different things to different people, it is shorthand for a different kind of adoption—one in which some kind of contact occurs between members of the birthfamily and the adoptive family. Thus, in this text, the term *open adoption* stands for any such contact after adoption.

Although researchers have studied openness in infant adoption (Grotevant & McRoy, 1998), U.S. researchers have made little systematic study of openness in child welfare adoptions (for an exception, see Frasch, Brooks, & Barth, 2000). Most of the arguments to support openness in these adoptions are philosophical, focusing on the benefits to children in coping with separation and loss. Such arguments generally assume the child is being adopted outside his or her family. Thus, it is important to connect children to their birthfamily to increase their understanding of the loss, to help with their sense of identity (particularly in children adopted across race or culture), and to provide ongoing access to information important to the child's physical and mental health.

The most common type of argument about contact centers on the perceived benefit to child well-being. Open adoptions may maintain important attachment relationships in the child's life. Most children adopted through the child welfare system will have had meaningful relationships with their birthparents and other family members and may have formed relationships with other caregivers. Whether contact after adoption maintains relationships or creates them, it is thought that contact reduces the child's sense of loss. Openness in adoption also acknowledges the birthfamily as an important part of the child's identity. Acceptance of and contact with birthparents is thought to validate their importance and reduce the child's sense of shame or responsibility for the separation.

For older children, the promise of openness may support their acceptance of adoption. In addition, ongoing contact with birthfamily members may serve the child's evolving understanding of why he or she came to be adopted. Seeing (and ultimately understanding) the limitations of birthparents may help the child counter fantasies and accept that the birthparent could not adequately meet the child's needs. Some adoption theorists argue that the more secrecy families have about birthparents, the greater the child's need to fantasize (Sorosky, Baran, & Pannor, 1989). When children can directly observe the reasons removal was warranted, they may not need to act out a negative image of their birthparents (Silverstein & Roszia, 1999).

Open adoption arrangements may also increase the likelihood that children will attach to their adoptive parents. Such connections are promoted when birthparents are involved in the transition to adoption, particularly if they support the adoption. Ongoing contact promotes continuity and minimizes loyalty conflicts. In the best of circumstances, openness in adoption "can help promote the child's ability to trust, feel optimistic about life, and establish positive relationships" (Silverstein & Roszia, 1999, p. 640).

Kin adoptions provide "natural experiments" in openness. By definition, they keep children connected to at least part of their birthfamilies. It is less

**Table 8.1**
Birthparent Contact (in percentages)

| Rating | Relative | Foster | Matched |
|---|---|---|---|
| Very often (weekly) | 21 | 0 | 1 |
| Often (about once a month) | 20 | 4 | 3 |
| Sometimes (a few times a year) | 23 | 9 | 5 |
| Rarely (once a year or less) | 17 | 10 | 7 |
| Never | 20 | 77 | 86 |

Note. $\chi^2 = 480.73$; $p < .001$.

clear if the other benefits ascribed to open adoption fit in kin adoption. For example, advocates of open adoption argue that contact strengthens the adoptive mother's sense of entitlement, making clear the differences between the parent who cares for the child from day to day and the parent who created the child. Is this more or less likely in kin adoptions? Some practitioners suggest that roles and boundaries are more complicated in kinship adoption. What are the ramifications of the grandmother becoming the mother? Of the mother becoming the sister? What conflicts may arise when a cousin becomes a brother? Although, historically, many families have managed such issues without outside intervention, such as when grandparents informally took in and raised grandchildren, what happens when the state requires the termination of parental rights and their formal transfer to the caregiving relative? Given the assumption that children benefit from adoption by relatives, do we adequately prepare kin adopters for the shift in relationships that can accompany formal adoption? Clearly much more needs to be understood about adoption by kin.

## Birthfamily Contact by Type of Adoption

One of the perceived benefits of adoption by kin is the greater likelihood that children will have access to birthparents and siblings. Indeed, kin respondents to the survey were far more likely to report that their child had contact with birthparents and siblings than were foster or, especially, matched families (see Table 8.1).

**Table 8.2**
Extent of Contact with Birthsiblings Placed Elsewhere (in percentages)

| Rating | Relative | Foster | Matched |
|---|---|---|---|
| Very often | 26 | 4 | 3 |
| Often | 17 | 9 | 4 |
| Sometimes | 27 | 19 | 15 |
| Rarely | 13 | 17 | 12 |
| Never | 18 | 52 | 66 |

Of children adopted by relatives, 80% had at least some contact with birthparents. Even in these homes, however, 37% of children never or rarely had contact with their birthparents. Birthparent contact was much less likely in both foster and matched homes ($\chi^2$ = 83.60, $p$ < .001).

Of cases in which contact did occur, children adopted by relatives were most likely to have in-person contact with birthparents. This was true in 73% of relative adopters with contact and 50% of foster parent adoptions. For matched families, in the 27 families in which any contact occurred, letters, photos, or phone contacts were the most common types.

Children in kinship care who had siblings in other placements were much more likely to see their siblings than children in other types of families ($\chi^2$ = 46.26, $p$ < .001), as shown in Table 8.2. Of these children, 70% had at least some regular contact with brothers and sisters and 43% saw their siblings often or very often. Only 32% of children adopted by foster parents and 22% of those adopted in matched families had contact with their siblings at least some of the time. When contact with siblings did occur, it was most often in person for all family types.

As in the case of birthparents and siblings, children adopted by relatives also visited other birthrelatives more often than children in other adoption types ($\chi^2$ = 619.57, $p$ < .001). Parents reported contact with other birthfamily members as occurring often or very often in 60% of relative adoption cases and sometimes (defined as *a few times a year*) in 20%. Children adopted by

**Table 8.3**

Effect of Birthfamily Contact (in percentages)

| | RELATIVE | | | FOSTER | | | MATCHED | | |
| --- | B | S | O | B | S | O | B | S | O |
| Harmful | 12 | 3 | 4 | 22 | 7 | 14 | 33 | 16 | 12 |
| Mixed | 53 | 24 | 20 | 55 | 44 | 44 | 33 | 51 | 33 |
| Helpful | 36 | 74 | 76 | 23 | 49 | 42 | 33 | 33 | 55 |

Note. B = birthparent; S = sibling; O = other.

foster parents had contact often or very often with other birthfamily members in only 5% of cases, and sometimes in 9% of them.

Those children matched with their adoptive parents were least likely to have contact with other birthfamily members. Parents reported such contact occurred often or very often in only 2% of cases, and occasional contact occurred in 9% of cases. In each type of adoption, when contact with other kin than birthparents and siblings did occur, it was likely to be in person.

Just because contact was allowed, does not mean it was uniformly welcomed. The survey asked those parents whose children did have contact to rate its effect on children, and Table 8.3 shows their responses. Both relative and matched parents saw contact with other birthrelatives (not birthparents or siblings) as having the most positive effect. Foster adoptive parents rated sibling contact as more helpful than other types of birthfamily contact. Relative adopters rated sibling contact as helpful nearly as often as they rated contact with other relatives positively. Overall, contact with birthparents was rated as least helpful. In several cases, contact with birthparents was judged to be harmful. This was more likely to be the case, however, for foster and matched adoptive parents than for relatives ($\chi^2 = 20.91$, $p < .001$).

The survey did not capture the reasons that contact does or does not occur. It is likely that relative adopters themselves have contact with members of the child's birthfamily, thus children have better opportunities for contact. Foster adoptive parents and, in particular, matched parents are less likely to know who their child's relatives are and where they may live. Furthermore, foster and matched adoptive parents are much more likely to see contact, particularly with birthparents, as having a negative effect on the child.

**Table 8.4**
Comfort Level of Allowing Contact with Birthfamily (in percentages)

| Rating | Relative | Foster | Matched |
|---|---|---|---|
| Very comfortable | 45 | 24 | 17 |
| Comfortable | 29 | 29 | 28 |
| Somewhat uncomfortable | 19 | 25 | 23 |
| Very uncomfortable | 7 | 23 | 32 |

The survey also did not determine the reasons contact with birthparents, siblings, or other family members was judged as harmful or helpful. Additional study of the nature of postadoption contact across family type would yield information about the benefits, as well as the drawbacks, of contact.

The survey asked parents to rate their general level of comfort with contact between children and birthfamily members (see Table 8.4). This question better captures general attitudes about contact. Both parents whose children did not have contact and those whose children did answered the question.

Relatives reported that they were or would be comfortable with contact much more often than other adopters—74% of relatives, compared with 53% of foster parents and 45% of matched adoptive parents were comfortable with contact ($\chi^2$ = 103.53, $p$ < .001). Again, the nature of survey questions does not explain why this is so—whether, for example, relatives have more experience with contact and, therefore, see it as benign, or whether other adopters have more reason to fear contact.

In summary, children adopted by relatives are more likely to have contact with members of their birthfamilies than children adopted into foster or matched homes. Relatives also are more comfortable allowing contact with birthfamily members and rate the effects of contact more positively than foster or matched adoptive parents do.

# References

Frasch, K. M., Brooks, D., & Barth, R. P. (2000). Openness and contact in foster care adoptions: An eight year follow-up. *Family Relations, 49*, 435–446.

Grotevant, H. D., & McRoy, R. G. (1998). *Openness in adoption: Exploring family connections.* Thousand Oaks, CA: Sage.

Silverstein, D., & Roszia, S. K. (1999). Openness: A critical component of special needs adoption. *Child Welfare, 78*, 637–651.

Sorosky, A., Baran, A., & Pannor, R. (1989). *The adoption triangle.* San Antonio, TX: Corona.

REFERENCES

# CHAPTER NINE

# Services Used and Services Needed by Kin, Foster, and Matched Parents

Most families participating in this study used some services related to their adopted children's needs. Given that relative adopters consistently identified fewer problems, it is not surprising that they were less likely to have used services than either foster or matched adoptive parents. Table 9.1 reports the most commonly used services. The most commonly used service across adoption types was counseling for the child. Of the children adopted by relatives, 32% had received counseling, compared with 48% of children adopted by foster parents and 58% of children in matched homes.

The survey also asked families about barriers to receiving help. Of relative adoptive parents, 32% identified barriers, whereas 47% of foster parents and 50% of matched parents did. The survey presented parents with a list of possible barriers and gave them the opportunity to list others. On every item but one, foster parents and matched parents were more likely to report a problem. That item was "Do not know how to find out about available services." Of relative parents, 19% identified this as a barrier, as did 15% of foster and 14% of matched adopters.

Other barriers that parents commonly identified were, "Dentists who accept the medical card" (identified by 23% of relatives, 37% of foster parents, and 45% of matched parents), "Doctors who accept the medical card (16%, 29%, and 39%, respectively), and "Services are too far away from where I live" (10%, 15%, and 16%, respectively).

Difficulties in finding dentists and doctors who accept the Medicaid card were the most commonly identified needs in both foster and matched parent

**Table 9.1**
Services Previously Used (in percentages)

| Service | Relative | Foster | Matched |
|---|---|---|---|
| Child counseling*** | 34 | 48 | 58 |
| Family counseling*** | 21 | 35 | 49 |
| Parent support group*** | 12 | 24 | 36 |
| Adoption assistance worker* | 16 | 24 | 33 |
| Original agency* | 10 | 14 | 28 |
| Child support group* | 9 | 13 | 18 |

*$p < .05$. ***$p < .001$.

adopters. Twenty percent of foster parents and matched parents also reported this difficulty with counselors. This was much less often the case among relative adopters, however—only 6% reported this difficulty ($\chi^2 = 480.73$; $p < .001.e = 43.92$, $p < .001$).

## Concerns of Relative Adopters

Parents completing the survey had several opportunities to identify service needs and make recommendations. This section addresses the particular concerns of relative adoptive parents.

Relative adoptive parents offered powerful insights into the satisfactions and challenges of being an adoptive parent to a child to whom one is related. Many parents took the opportunity to talk about the importance of adoption. One grandmother wrote:

> An adoptive parent must have love, patience and understanding. It helps to be able to feel what they feel. I was raised without parents. I experienced [it] and know what it feels like. I love my grandchildren, and if they weren't my adoptive grandchildren I would do the same for others.

Several parents noted the pleasure their children had brought into their lives. Many comments echoed the sentiments of these parents:

Go ahead and adopt! I wouldn't change a thing. I love my son very much. He is my pride and joy.

My two grandchildren have fulfilled my life. They are very helpful to me and I thank God for them!

Others poignantly described the circumstances that brought children to adoption in the first place. One grandmother wrote:

My daughter was on the street running. I have always had her kids, most of the time. She's dead and gone now from AIDS. I really miss her. I wish she could see her kids—she has four children. I got two, a white lady got one, and one got killed at 20 years old.

Some parents described some of the complications of relative adoption and offered suggestions based on their experiences:

If family adoptions are done a lot, I would recommend that all the family get counseling together. And that when the child is with one family member, then removed and placed with another family member, they should be told why and get counseling for them. Our family has been split ever since the placement. There is some contact, but at Christmas our child goes to one family get-together, and we and our other children are not invited. Families, in my opinion, have to be very strong, loving, and understanding to go through with family adoption.

Adoption by grandparents is confusing for the child, and the [birth] parents never go away. No agency should tell you they'll remove your child if you're not comfortable with adoption.

I had my son since he came home from the hospital. One day, I am sure he is going to ask me why I have him! "Why didn't my grandmother take me after my mother died? Where is my father? Why doesn't he come and see me? Why are my brothers somewhere else? Why? Why? Why?" Families need help explaining all this.

[As a grandmother] I will say, things change with children, and you forget how you raised yours, and then you have to start all over again.

When parents made recommendations, their most common request was for ongoing support and information. Many parents described needing to have someone to talk to, to get advice, to learn about existing services, or to be referred for counseling or other help. A common recommendation was that the supervising agency should be available to help for a longer period—perhaps throughout the child's growing up years.

Several parents noted that problems can arise after the adoption, often tied to their child's earlier history, and that ongoing help is important:

If parents adopt a substance abuse child, tell them—repeat and warn them—about the slow learning of the child. [And] give help 24/7.

I think there should be more child care and group sessions available easily for families who adopt children, and also way more help. Because it's like when you adopt the children you're on your own.

I think we need more support services and at least once a year, call, written, or in-person communication from [the] adoption agency to check on [the] status of family and child services. We need very well-trained professionals.

Have someone knowledgeable in how to help us when we call for help. When I first adopted my grandchildren, I called the adoption assistance worker for help, [and] she knew even less than I the right people to talk to. I ended up calling 10–12 agencies in order to find the right people to talk to.

One mother was quite specific, asking:

1. What do you do when your kids start going to jail?
2. When they get kicked out of school?
3. They are sassy?

4. You can't trust them out in the neighborhood?

5. Who do you call for this information?

Several parents identified the need for a list of services that is regularly updated and specific to their community:

> Better and easier access to information about adoption issues, adopted children's issues, parenting, etc., would be wonderful. Internet access—it would be immediate access at the time it is most needed. [DCFS] could send out a list of good websites. Also, adoptive parents should be informed of all services available and how to reach them. It takes a lot of digging to get what we need sometimes.

> Ongoing communication with updates about available services from the agency [is needed]. There are many areas of assistance I do not know how to access but have only heard of through word of mouth.

Although the most frequently identified need was for information, referral, and support after adoption, many parents identified specific needs. The most common among these for relative adoptive parents was the need for more income or in-kind support that would allow them to improve their housing situation, more easily purchase food, or provide other basics.

> [We need] medication, clothes, beds, dressers. And a better, larger home and ways to help families get what they need.

The particular problems of single parents and older adoptive parents came through in several comments:

> When a single parent adopts children, they are going to need help with the support of the children. The board money is good and helps, but it is not enough if the parent works, but for little money and has a mortgage and all the bills. The working parent can't afford to pay for a sitter until she or he gets off work. Please help them with child care.

Help more with more money for low-income families. All I have is my Social Security check, and after the bills are paid, there just isn't enough left, even with the adoption subsidy to get him the things he needs....Low-income families are at a severe disadvantage over higher income families.

More money. We do not get enough money to go anywhere. I can't take them places where I would like to. Because when we get through paying bills, there is nothing left. I would like to take them out of town sometimes, places where they have never seen. A vacation in the summertime when school is out. Most of our money go on food. I spent from $400 on food alone—they eat a lot!

Now that my girl is 10 years old, I need more money to feed her and for clothes. I am retired. I use my money on her.

## Needs for Additional Services

Relative adoptive parents also identified the need for additional services—some because they could not afford them, and some because they did not know where to find them. For the former, the most commonly expressed need was for child care, followed by camp and recreational programs, transportation, and respite. Some parents noted that their children lost benefits such as child care, summer camp, or tutoring when they adopted, although the need remained:

I realize we do get subsidy for the children. However, child care while I work is needed. I do not qualify for public assistance. The subsidy is great, but child care alone is anywhere from $100 to $200 a week.

It would be helpful if before and afterschool day care monies were included in the adoption [subsidy]. I believe the fact that working parents suddenly acquire exorbitant day care expenses is a deterrent to adoption.

Parents identified recreational needs as well. As was the case with child care, parents identified this as something they had difficulty paying for:

It would be good when submitting [subsidy] plans to document or make space for social activities, i.e., camps, sports, etc. These children must learn how to function socially in today's world. The basic budget does not take this into consideration.

Some parents also asked for respite, although they did not use the term specifically:

No one will watch my child. I can barely get a break. I hurt so bad and so long from this situation. I almost lost my husband of 30 years....I would love a week's vacation. It took me two months to fill out this form because I didn't like what was happening to me and my family and I didn't want to lie.

Being the grandmother/adoptive parent to five siblings, I could certainly appreciate a two-[or] three-day vacation or break period. With pay.

Given the very low incomes of kin adopters, and the fact that they are more likely to adopt sibling groups than other adopters, it is not surprising that kin adoptive parents sought help paying for services. Although several parents requested financial help, some reported on the lack of needed services or their frustration in finding them:

Foster care and adopted children with special needs that suffer from ADHD, for example, should have their own day care centers with trained professionals to deal with these children, rather than having them kicked out of one day care facility to the next.

Relative adopters also made recommendations about the services they received prior to adoption, the need to speed up the adoption process, and the importance of keeping siblings together. Most concerns about casework prior to the adoption concerned the need for more contact from the agency, better information about subsidy and services after adoption, and the need for full information about the child's history:

I would tell you to make sure the things workers tell you are true about services you can get once you adopted a child. I love my babies very much, but it is very hard when you can't pay for services that your child needs to help become a better person. Caseworkers tell you things that [are] not true. When you call for different services, they tell you it's your child now, you have to pay for these services. They can't help. But you people want people to adopt child[ren] with the little money you give. We need help.

My recommendations are to have the birthparents fill out a family medical history to let us know what possible illnesses our children may be in danger of having. Also to let adoptive parents know if the birthparents used drugs while being pregnant with child. My son has bad eyes, which the doctor says is inherited and I don't know. I don't know if he has diabetes in his immediate family or not. I am a distant cousin so my genes are different.

[Workers should] tell more information about what is to come—what effects it [maltreatment] might have on the child.

## Support for Kin Adopters

Although kin adopters share many of the same concerns as foster and matched parents, they have important differences. Kin adopters tend to have much lower incomes, suggesting that subsidies (both financial support and other services) are very important to their families' well-being. Kin adopters also are much more likely to be African American. Most are single parents. Some innovative programs indicate these families may be best served through natural helping systems and paraprofessional home visitors.

California's Kinship Support Network, although in place for relative foster parents, offers some ideas for meeting the needs of relative adopters. The Edgewood Center for Children and Families in San Francisco developed this system of services to meet the special needs of kinship caregivers (Cohan & Cooper, 1999). The agency offers Grandparents Who Care groups to support grandparents, most of whom are single and African American, who are stressed by the responsibility of caring for grandchildren. Through observation of the support groups, agency workers identified needs among these caregivers: respite from caregiving responsibility, recreational opportunities for children, and the need for more respect from helping professionals. A formal assessment of group members added the following concerns:

- monetary needs,
- peer support,
- help with challenging behavior problems of children,
- confusion about public agency bureaucracy, and
- concern about their children's drug use.

In response to these concerns, Edgewood developed the Kinship Support Network, a community-based approach, under contract with the public Department of Human Services. This allowed services to be provided to families without the stigma of public service involvement, a concern that had been raised by parents.

The assessments Edgewood conducted found that mistrust or uncertainly about the formal public service system inhibited kin caregivers. Edgewood hired elderly African American and Hispanic grandparents from the communities in which families lived to provide advice and link families with needed resources and monitor their progress, "assuming the roles of second and third generations in the informal extended family support system" (Cohan & Cooper, 1999, p. 316). Community-based workers, who became advocates, information givers, and sources of support, were a critically important part of the service.

The comments of many kin adopters in our study suggested they hoped or expected that the support and information provided before adoption would continue after finalization. Furthermore, they often reported they did not know where to get help or how to determine if they were eligible for services. The peer-support model offered by Edgewood is an instructive model to consider in providing a supportive, low-cost service to relative adopters.

Another difference between kin adopters and most others adopting children with special needs is the presence of birthfamily members in the child's life. Most children adopted by relatives will have regular contact with their birthparents and siblings. Although this has advantages for children, in some cases, it poses problems. Conflict within the kinship system, confusion about roles, and discomfort among relative adoptive parents about setting limits on birthparents can all be more complex in a relative adoption. Some have suggested mediation, a nonadversarial process of negotiated consensus that accommodates the needs of all parties, as a culturally appropriate strategy for families of color. Wilhelmus (1998) discussed mediation as a model for kinship care services and its utility in solving problems between public agencies and families. The same process may be useful to families sorting out the complexities of kinship adoption. Wilhemus argued for service providers to become skillful in identifying trusted community members to serve as mediators or to train mediators from a community to serve this function.

## Accounting for the Positive and Negative Outcomes in Relative Adoption

Relative adoption does appear to be very successful, based on the responses of relative adoptive parents in this study. A small subset of relative adoptions, however, are very troubled. This section considers the characteristics that may make kin adoption more successful, as well as the factors that account for difficulties when they are present.

## Success in Kinship Adoption

Relative adoptive parents report far fewer problems raising their children, and they rate their adopted children as less difficult on many measures. Even when children adopted by kin do have serious problems, relatives are less likely to see them as problematic than foster parent adopters or, in particular, matched parents. Furthermore, kin adoptive parents are less likely to report they would not adopt their child again, knowing what they now know.

What accounts for these differences? Children adopted by relatives appear to be less troubled. They have lower BPI scores, fewer adverse factors in their preadoption history, and fewer special needs. In addition, children adopted by relatives were somewhat younger at the time of survey completion than those adopted by foster or matched parents (11.8 vs. 12.0 and 13.0 years). Studies have reported that behavior problems among adopted children increase with age (see, for example, Rosenthal & Groze, 1994). Even when researchers control for age, however, relatives report their children are less difficult to raise and have fewer behavior problems.

The fact that kin-adopted children have fewer reported problems needs consideration as well. Is it that these children brought fewer problems with them to adoption or that they are less troubled because they are cared for by relatives? It is difficult to ascertain this from this survey. Some differences in the situations of children adopted by relatives and children adopted by other people bear further investigation.

First, children adopted by relatives have been with them more consistently since removal from their birthfamilies. Children adopted by relatives averaged less than 10 months in care before joining their eventual adoptive families. Children adopted by foster parents averaged more than a year in care and matched children averaged more than two years. As a result, children adopted by relatives had fewer moves in care and were less likely to have experienced an adoption disruption.

Second, kin-adopted children were likely to have access to their birthfamilies. Children in relative homes were much more likely to have contact with birthparents and siblings in other placements. Even if they do not have contact or it is rare, as is the case in 37% of relative adoptions, children have a connection to their family of origin through their relationship with members of their birthfamilies that may protect against some of the identity struggles and loss that are associated with permanent separation from birthfamilies.

Third, relative adopters report they know more about their children's backgrounds. Thus they may be more aware of complications that their children may face or be better prepared to respond to those complications. They may be better positioned to help children understand what has happened to them.

Fourth, relatives may be more tolerant of difficulties in their children. For example, among those children with high BPI scores (15 or more), relatives were more likely to be satisfied with the adoption and feel closer to their child than other adopters. Relative adopters were much less likely to rate the child as difficult to raise. Past research has linked high expectations for child achievement to less positive adoption outcomes. Relative adopters are much more likely than other adopters to have limited educational attainment. Compared with more educated adoptive parents, these parents may be more accepting of children as they are and less likely to demand more from them than they are capable of, particularly in terms of educational achievement.

Finally, it may be that race, rather than kinship, accounts for the better outcomes of children adopted by relatives. These children are much more likely to be African American than those adopted by nonrelatives. Overall, African

American children generally had fewer problems than white children. For example, African American children had mean BPI scores of 10.39, compared with 14.08 for white children. The parents of African American children were less likely to rate their children as difficult to raise than white parents (23% vs. 33%), and they were less likely to report dissatisfaction with the adoption (3% vs. 8%). Furthermore, African American parents were more likely to report they were very close to their children (92% vs. 80%). African American children adopted by relatives had lower average BPI scores than white children adopted by relatives (8.8 vs. 13.4). Thus, it may be race rather than kinship adoption that is the protective factor.

In an attempt to shed further light on this question, the researchers compared African American children adopted by kin and African American children adopted by nonkin. If it were race alone, rather than adoption by relatives, that accounted for fewer behavior problems, then scores for African American children should be similar despite type of adoption. African American children adopted by kin, however, had significantly lower BPI scores (average of 8.9) than African American children adopted by nonkin (average of 11.0).

The researchers then examined BPI scores in light of the types of maltreatment children had experienced. An examination of the number of types of previous maltreatment and BPI scores indicated that African American children adopted by kin did indeed fare better when they had no maltreatment or only one type of maltreatment in their past ($F = 6.53$, $p = .01$). African American children adopted by relatives who had experienced only one or no types of maltreatment had significantly fewer behavior problems than African American children with the same levels of maltreatment who were adopted by nonkin. These differences disappear, however, for children experiencing two or more types of maltreatment. Thus, the benefits of kinship adoption diminish as the number of types of maltreatment increases.

Much is left to untangle in our understanding of adoption by kin. Are relatives more positive about most aspects of adoption because their children are less troubled, or are their children less troubled because they were taken in by relatives? Is it adoption by kin per se that accounts for better outcomes among these children, or is it that these children already had close relationships with kin caregivers? Why is kin adoption predominantly African American adoption? And why do white children adopted by kin have more behavior problems than African American children adopted by kin? The growing emphasis on kin adoption requires that the field of child welfare examine these questions in further research.

## Characteristics of Troubled Relative Adoptions

Although relatives generally reported higher levels of satisfaction with adoption, some relative adoptive families did report having children who posed challenges. As indicated earlier, 25% of relative adopters rated their children as difficult or very difficult to raise. In addition, parents in 24% of the relative homes rated their children as having serious behavior problems (score of 15 or more on BPI). Of relative adopters, 23 (4%) reported that, knowing what they now know, they probably would not adopt their child again.

The few children whose kin adoptive parents reported they would not adopt them again shared more characteristics with the general group of children in matched adoptions than they did with other relative-adopted children. They were also similar to children who would not be adopted again in the other two groups. For example, similarity existed across all groups for BPI scores among those whose parents reported they would not adopt them again.

Among the small number of relative adopters who probably would not or definitely would not adopt again, children had more serious problems than relative-adopted children generally. For example, 76% had experienced serious neglect, and 81% had been prenatally exposed to alcohol or drugs. These children were more likely to have each adverse factor item than the general group of children adopted by relatives, with the exception of sexual abuse. These parents also reported they were less well prepared for adoption than relatives as a whole.

## Conclusion

This examination of families receiving adoption assistance by type of adoption yields insight into variations within special-needs adoptions. Parental responses to questions on this survey offer affirmation of the practice of placing children with relatives when feasible. Relative adoptive parents consistently described their children's functioning more positively, expressed greater satisfaction, and reported feeling closer to their children. Foster children generally fared well too, although their parents reported more difficulty than relative adoptive parents.

This study points out not only the benefits of kin adoption but the importance of paying particular attention to the needs of matched adoptive families. Matched adoptive parents generally report more problems. For example, every indicator of school problems in Table 7.2 was highest among children in matched families. When one considers that these children also spent more time in the child welfare system before being placed in their adoptive homes, and they did not have the advantage of previous relationships with their new families, it is not surprising that they and their families had more difficulty.

Although all families need information, and many need support, matched families deserve our particular attention. Variation exists, of course, in matched adoptions as well, and some families reported few behavior problems and high satisfaction with adoption. Matched families clearly struggled the most, however. It is critically important to provide information and support to these families after adoption.

It is necessary to consider that kin adoptions, although the best choice for many children, also have limitations. In this study, kin adopters had much lower incomes than other adopters and very low incomes generally. When asked for recommendations, they were more likely to request additional income or support for child care, transportation, or recreation for their children. Low family incomes may constrain children's opportunities. As Magruder (1994) noted in his study of relative adopters in California, "For some children the benefits of kinship placement may be offset to some degree by the barriers the families' limited resources may place on the fulfillment of the child's potential" (p. 131). Furthermore, variations in kin adoption exist, and we need to be careful to assess and respond to the particular needs of different kin adoptive families.

# References

Cohan, J. D., & Cooper, B. A. (1999). Kinship support network: Edgewood's program model and client characteristics. *Children and Youth Services Review, 21,* 311–338.

Magruder, J. (1994). Characteristics of relative and non-relative adoptions by California public adoption agencies. *Children and Youth Services Review, 16,* 123–131.

Rosenthal, J. A., & Groze, V. K. (1994). A longitudinal study of special-needs adoptive families. *Child Welfare, 73,* 689–706.

Wilhelmus, M. (1998). Mediation in kinship care: Another step in the provision of culturally relevant child welfare services. *Social Work, 43*(4), 117–126.

# PART III
## CONCLUSIONS AND RECOMMENDATIONS

# Chapter Ten

# Conclusions and Recommendations

## Study Limitations

This study examines child adjustment and family life at a single point in time. We cannot know from the data what the future holds for these children. Two longitudinal studies conducted with child welfare adoptive families suggest that the problems of some children with special needs intensify as they age and that parental satisfaction declines somewhat over time (Groze, 1996; Rosenthal & Groze, 1994). A study of the behavior problems of international adoptees over a three-year period reported that this increase of behavior problem scores among the adoptees was not characteristic of children in the general population (Verhulst & Versluis-den Bieman, 1995). Thus, the positive overall findings need to be tempered by the possibility that challenges for many families may increase as children age.

Although this study is based on more than 1,300 responses, this represents only 34% of families in the sample. Thus, we cannot be sure that these responses are representative of the experiences of all families. Although families appear to be similar on some dimensions (geographic location, child age), they are different on others, particularly child race, with somewhat fewer African American children included among the respondents in this study than in the population of children adopted from the state's child welfare system.

A final concern is that the findings are based exclusively on parent responses. As is typically the case with large surveys, no independent validation of parental perspectives exists. The use of a standardized instrument on child behavior problems provides a somewhat more objective measure on this dimension, although the items of this instrument are still dependent on parental perceptions of child behaviors. The findings of this study should be considered in light of these limitations. It is clear that additional study is needed on children and their families after adoption.

## Primary Findings and Related Recommendations

In this study, the majority of adopted children whose families receive adoption assistance are faring well. Although many children were seriously affected by early experiences of impermanence and maltreatment, most are resilient and function successfully in their families and communities. Perhaps most important, they are living in families who feel close to them and are committed to them. This is evident from parental responses in almost all families responding to the survey, even when children were struggling with serious behavioral and emotional problems, physical disabilities, chronic illness, or mental retardation.

Evidence of the overall positive adjustment of these families is plentiful. There is a high level of parental satisfaction with their adoptions among respondents—only 9% responded negatively. On questions related to children's mental health and their functioning in school and at home, children's overall adjustment was rated as excellent or good in 69% to 89% of cases.

Again, it is important to remember that these findings represent the adjustment of the children and their families at one point in time. Some of the children who currently function satisfactorily may develop difficulties later. Others who are struggling may improve. Because many conditions manifest themselves over the course of a child's development, it is difficult to know when a child is young what challenges he may face at later ages. For example, one mother wrote on the survey that her 7-year-old son was doing just fine, but said that he had told her recently that he heard voices. Mental illness and some other disorders frequently are not evident at the time the child is adopted or during much of his or her childhood.

Many families reported that they need few services beyond financial subsidies, Medicaid, and information. A sizeable proportion of children, however, had very high levels of behavioral and emotional problems. This is based on the finding that about 40% of these adopted children's BPI scores rank in the top 10% of normed scores. This high level of problems poses an ongoing risk to these children's positive adjustments in all areas of their lives. These families need periodic assistance in addressing these problems.

It appears that 10% to 15% of the children have very serious problems that may threaten family stability. Generally, these were the children whose parents described them as very difficult to raise. These families are likely to need additional supports and services on an ongoing basis.

Included in this latter group is a small minority of children whose problems will remain complex no matter what services are provided. These children have chronic and severe medical conditions, autism, severe emotional disturbances, significant mental retardation, brain disorders, and other serious conditions. Such families need more than ongoing supportive services. They will likely need help in connecting with specialized services and, in a small number of cases, assistance in placing their children in residential facilities.

The findings of this study suggest a number of ways the system of supports and benefits might be improved. The following section summarizes the primary findings in each key area of the survey and presents recommendations linked to these findings. As might be expected, some overlap exists between recommendations in the various areas.

## Training and Other Preparation for Adoption

Parents who received training found it helpful in nearly all cases. Less than half of all responding families, however, reported receiving adoption training prior to the adoption of their child. Some of the issues parents raised in other sections of the survey, such as meeting the challenges of raising a child with FAS or finding educational resources, might have been addressed in training.

In addition to training, workers need to provide other types of adoption preparation to children and families. The regression analysis indicates that being fully prepared for adoption is the most important parent factor in predicting child adjustment. It is important to note that this is a retrospective response. Current difficulties may shape parent attitudes about their preparation.

Sound preparation has many aspects, including:

- sharing complete information,
- helping parents understand how the particular loss and trauma experiences that their child experienced may manifest over the course of the child's development,
- informing families of available postadoption services and how to obtain ongoing support and other types of help,

- educating parents about adoption issues and the emergence of issues over the developmental child and family lifecycle,
- addressing concerns about the birthfamily and helping assess when contact with the birthfamily or other significant attachment figures is in the child's best interest,
- helping develop skills to respond effectively to children's emotional and behavioral needs,
- helping children make sense of the important events in their past through lifebook work and other strategies,
- performing disengagement work with the child and birthfamily and other significant attachment figures, and
- supporting the child in making or cementing emotional connections to adoptive parents.

Although parents generally were satisfied with their children's preparation for adoption, they reported that some basic casework practices were not routinely provided. Doing lifebook work with children, connecting the child and family to previous foster parents, phasing children into the adoptive home slowly in matched adoptions, and directly working with children to prepare them for adoption occurred in fewer than half of all cases, with lifebook work conducted in only 25%.

This study supported the importance of thorough background information (and echoed the findings of Rosenthal, Groze, & Morgan, 1996). Parents raised concerns about full disclosure and explanation about what a complicated early history or a medical condition might mean for the child in later life. Many parents (45%) reported that they did not receive information about their child's background in writing.

## Recommendations

All adoptive parents need to receive training related to adoption issues. Even when parents have an existing relationship with their child, adoption poses issues that are different from raising birthchildren or foster children. This is particularly true of children who cope not only with adoption, but also with interrupted attachments and previous maltreatment. More extensive training on specific topics should be required of all parents adopting a child who has or is strongly suspected of having the following concerns:

- attachment difficulties;
- a history of FAS or prenatal drug exposure;
- significant deprivation in early life;
- serious abuse, both physical and sexual;
- oppositional and defiant behavior problems; or
- symptoms evidencing mental illness.

Furthermore, parents raising a child of a race or ethnicity different from their own should receive training specific to promoting positive racial identity and coping with racism.

Parents should receive all information about the child and the child's birthfamily and extended family that legally can be provided. This information should be presented both verbally and in written form. The written document should remain part of the child's permanent file so that it can be retrieved if parents misplace it. The document should provide information about the likely ramifications of physical and mental health diagnoses and past experiences (e.g., the meaning of FAS for a child's long-term development). Because many workers may struggle with composing such documents, boilerplates for different special conditions might be created for workers to adapt, or specific informational booklets might be created to give parents with children having specific difficulties. Informational brochures for adoptive parents on some of these topics are available from some agencies and organizations.

## Children's Adjustments at Home

Parents were less likely to evaluate their children's overall adjustments at home as problematic than their adjustments at school or their overall mental health. Parents often rated even children with serious problems, such as autism or severe medical conditions, as having good adjustments at home. More than two-thirds of parents, however, identified some concern or service need related to the children's functioning at home. The primary needs related to professional counseling or management of the children's behavior problems.

Because of the high levels of behavior problems among approximately half these children, behavioral management and effective interventions related to these behaviors at the earliest possible stage in the children's development are primary needs.

The adoption literature suggests that many negative behaviors may be coping mechanisms for children who have experienced interrupted attachments and trauma (Delaney & Kunstal, 1993; Keck & Kupecky, 1995; Smith & Howard, 1999). Hence, a child who has experienced repeated losses or maltreatment at the hands of a parent may act out to distance caregivers, or a child who has felt helpless to defend himself or herself against repeated abuse may exhibit senseless lying or angry defiance to maintain control and a sense of personal power. These coping mechanisms often appear to be very resistant to change, and typical behavior management interventions may have little effect. Even experienced parents may not have the repertoire of parenting skills to effectively modify children's negative behaviors. Clinicians advocate the use of creative interventions for the parent to disengage from power struggles and respond in a firm but loving manner to the child's behaviors (Delaney & Kunstal, 1993; Keck & Kupecky, 1995).

The level of a child's behavior problems appears to be strongly related to other aspects of overall adoption adjustment. Hence, minimizing behavior problems as early as possible in the child's life would likely reduce problems in other areas as well.

This study suggests that there may be a negative effect on the relationships between spouses or partners when children have a high level of problems. The clinical literature discusses a "splitting" dynamic, in which an acting-out child divides authority figures or relates to one parent positively and one negatively. Adoptive mothers in families seeking counseling often report that the child reacts much more negatively to them than to their husband. Consequently, fathers may have a more positive experience with the child and be less than sympathetic to the mother's parenting frustrations. Also, parents often disagree about how to best cope with a child's problems or discipline the child. Parents with more disturbed children need to be made aware of this dynamic and the importance of maintaining a united front in their interactions with the child.

A small percentage of parents expressed a critical need for respite care for their children. Although this service is probably essential in a small minority of the cases reported in this study (10%–15%), when needed, it is extremely important to parents' ongoing ability to cope with child care demands. Many more families could benefit from respite services. Rosenthal et al. (1996) also found respite to be a valuable service in their follow-up study of 562 families who adopted children with special needs. More than 80% of the families in their study rated respite as very helpful, and more than two-thirds of parents whose children had significant behavior problems but did not receive respite saw it as a need.

## Recommendations

1. Training on behavioral management of children with high levels of behavior problems, particularly oppositional behaviors and behaviors stemming from prenatal alcohol or drug exposure, needs to be given to parents whose adopted children exhibit these behavioral problems. This training needs to be available both prior to adoption and throughout the course of the child's development.

   Some parents will absorb and be able to apply knowledge from training provided before they face specific problems; others will be motivated to participate in such training only if they are experiencing stress and perceive the training as a possible solution. Ideally, postadoption service providers would choose one or two excellent behavioral management or parenting curricula that address these behavioral issues. Training on teaching this content could be provided to support group leaders, people delivering adoption preparation services, and mental health providers.

   Ideally, this training for parents would be available using multiple modalities to reach those who need it: structured classes, support groups, and parent conferences or one-day workshops. Providing this content in written materials or videos through agency lending libraries may benefit those for whom travel is a barrier.

2. Respite care needs to be available to those parents with very intensive and stressful child care demands. Although many families can benefit from respite care, it can be a lifeline for parents with extremely heavy caregiving demands. This may be a very small percentage of families overall. Respite care, if available, may prevent the need for residential care for some children.

3. Because a high proportion of adoptive families have low incomes, it is vitally important to maintain the integrity and level of adoption subsidies. Subsidies may not be in jeopardy currently, but with the recent increase in adoptions and subsequent increase in costs, it could become a legislative issue. Advocates can use the

findings of this study to underscore the necessity of maintaining subsidies to these families. Subsidies appear to be of particular importance to kin adopters, whose incomes were significantly less than those of foster and matched adopters.

## Adjustments at School

School functioning was the area in which parents reported most often that children had difficulty. Slightly more than half of the parents reported that teachers had complained that their children's behaviors (such as ADHD and conduct problems) interfered with learning. Of the children, 40% received special education services for learning problems.

The majority of parents who made suggestions about education wanted tutoring services. Other parental concerns were related to obtaining appropriate assessments of children's needs and moving children into or out of special education. For about one-fourth of the children, suspensions and expulsions were an issue.

Some innovative programs that support the school performances of adopted children could serve as models. Adoptions Together, Inc., in Kensington, Maryland, developed one such program, Project Succeed, with funding from an adoption opportunities grant. This program provided training to teachers and school staff about adoption issues, telephone support, information and referrals for families with questions about their children's educations, an educational consultant for consultation and support to parents, and periodic workshops for parents on particular education-related topics.

### Recommendations

1. Families should be able to access the services of educational advocates who could inform families of their rights and directly assist families in navigating bureaucratic barriers. (For example, Illinois has developed an educational advocacy program for foster children that has been expanded to serve adopted children.) Educational advocates work with parents to ensure that children obtain the proper classroom placement and special services needed to address their educational needs. Ideally, the advocate is available to attend individual education plan conferences and appeal hearings with parents. In particular, children with multiple school suspensions may need such services.

2. Families need to receive information and training on educational issues. Many children struggle with learning disabilities, such as ADHD. Training efforts need to include strategies for parents to address children's educational issues.

3. For children with significant educational lags, tutoring is a critically needed resource. Children's experiences in the child welfare system often have exacerbated their educational deficits. Child welfare systems, therefore, need to explore existing avenues for families in need to obtain tutoring through other systems and work toward providing tutoring services to families who cannot obtain this service elsewhere. For example, Georgia's postadoption services include a tutoring program available to any child with a demonstrated need for educational assistance.

## Physical and Mental Health of Children

Although less than 10% of children in this study had serious medical problems, about 30% were reported as having special medical needs. Also, about two-thirds of families depended on Medicaid to meet their children's medical needs.

Of parents, 40% stated that their children had medical needs that were not being met. Parents frequently could not find dentists, doctors, or therapists who accept the Medicaid card. When providers can be found they are often at considerable distance from the family home. Furthermore, several parents raised concerns about the quality of care obtained through Medicaid. Parents also report difficulty in finding experts in areas such as FAS, ADHD, and attachment disorders.

In relation to children's mental health, 25% of respondents reported problematic levels of adjustment, and about 40% reported some needs in this area. Also, 12% of parents reported that children already had experienced psychiatric hospitalization or residential treatment. Primary problems in relation to children's mental health include accessing mental health providers, finding specialized treatments, and coping on a day-to-day basis with children's emotional and behavioral problems.

## Recommendations

1. Solving problems of access to quality providers who accept Medicaid cards is unlikely to be accomplished by the public child welfare agency alone. Although a larger effort is needed to correct the problem of supply, some of the problems could be addressed through the efforts of a medical advocate, based on the model of the educational advocate. Parents need a source of information, support, and occasional advocacy related to physical and mental health needs. They also need verbal and written information about their children's rights as Medicaid recipients. In addition, child welfare systems need to address system barriers, such as lengthy reimbursement periods, which may discourage providers from accepting Medicaid patients.

2. If such efforts are not already under way, states need to increase the pool of adoption-sensitive mental health providers by providing adoption-related training to interested mental health professionals. This training needs to have content related to understanding the issues affecting these children and families (attachment, loss, trauma, identity, common dynamics in troubled families, and others), as well as content on intervention techniques that address these problems. In addition, agencies need to pay attention to expanding the expertise of a pool of providers who can address very specialized needs. These would include treating reactive attachment disorder, diagnosing and treating children with severe trauma reactions (particularly those with neurological effects from trauma), and treating children with significant effects from prenatal alcohol or drug exposure.

3. Identify children who are at high risk for serious emotional and behavior problems and provide early intervention and more intensive postplacement services to these children and their families. Children with an adoption plan should be screened for risk factors and intervention plans should be articulated for children at significant risk for later problems. It is necessary to identify such risks early in children's developmental courses to maximize their chances for successful adjustment.

Possible risk factors for children include those listed on the first recommendation related to preparation: delays due to alcohol and drug exposure, an inability to give and receive affection, oppositional defiant behaviors, and a history of serious abuse. Other high-risk indicators include scoring high on BPI or another standardized behavioral measure and having a history of psychiatric hospitalization or symptoms of serious emotional disturbance.

In addition to the more extensive preparation and more intensive postplacement services offered in high-risk placements, the authors recommend that targeted families have an advocate in the child welfare system. This advocate could provide information, links to resources, or advocacy beyond the point of finalization.

## Children's Functioning in the Community

Although parents reported that most children were doing well in their neighborhoods and communities, slightly more than one in five parents expressed specific concerns about their children's abilities in this domain. Most of their concerns stemmed from developmental immaturities or problems of the child that affected their safety or ability to fit in with other children. Other parental concerns related to the risk to children of drugs and violence in their neighborhoods.

### Recommendations

1. As was the case with access to medical care, unsafe neighborhoods are a societal problem that cannot be solved by the public child welfare system alone. A small step is to work with families before placement or finalization to find safer housing. This kind of basic casework, not specifically tied to adoption work, may reduce risk for children in some families.

2. Workers need to develop recreational and mentoring programs for adopted children to address parental concerns related to children's functioning in the larger community. Traditional community groups do not accept many adopted children with developmental delays and behavior problems. Special social and recreational programs that provide appropriate structure and supervision for these children enable them to have successful social experiences.

## The Range of Postadoption Services

Most adoptive families may not need intensive services after their adoptions are finalized. The solutions parents desired, however, represent a continuum of postadoption services, including:

- a designated contact person the family can call with questions;
- a list of resources, including both community resources and statewide experts, related to key areas of need;
- newsletters and other information specific to parenting children with special needs;
- informational meetings for parents on specific topics of interest;
- support groups for parents and children;
- advocacy for parents who have difficulty meeting children's educational, health, and mental health needs;
- professional counseling services that address child and family needs;
- specialized professional treatment for children and families with specialized needs, such as attachment problems, FAS, and others;
- respite care for families who are struggling with very difficult child care situations; and
- residential treatment for those children who cannot be cared for at home.

## Conclusion

The findings of this study provide affirmation for efforts to achieve permanency for children through adoption. Despite complicated early life experiences, most children in this study are faring well in their homes, schools, and communities. Their parents are committed to them and feel close to them. Adoption has been a positive experience. Yet these children and their families face challenges, often tied to children's previous maltreatment and its manifestations.

As the number of adoptions of children with special needs increases, so too should our commitment to maintaining and strengthening these families. Systematic, comprehensive postadoption services are not yet available to most adoptive families. We need to commit ourselves to providing support to these families through a range of services both before and after adoption. It is hoped that this study can assist in the development of better preparation of children and adoptive parents and better postadoption support for them across the nation.

## References

Delaney, R. J., & Kunstal, F. R. (1993). *Troubled transplants: Unconventional strategies for helping disturbed foster and adopted children.* Portland, ME: National Child Welfare Resource Center for Management and Administration.

Groze, V. (1996). *Successful adoptive families: A longitudinal study of special needs adoption.* Westport, CT: Praeger.

Keck, G. C., & Kupecky, R. M. (1995). *Adopting the hurt child: Hope for families with special needs kids.* Colorado Springs, CO: Pinon Press.

Rosenthal, J. A., & Groze, V. K. (1994). A longitudinal study of special-needs adoptive families. *Child Welfare, 73,* 689–706.

Rosenthal, J. A., Groze, V., & Morgan, J. (1996). Services for families adopting children via public child welfare agencies: Use, helpfulness, and need. *Children and Youth Services Review, 18,* 163–182.

Smith, S. L., & Howard, J. H. (1999). *Promoting successful adoptions: Practice with troubled families.* Thousand Oaks, CA: Sage.

Verhulst, F. C., & Versluis-den Bieman, H. J. M. (1995). Developmental course of problem behaviors in adolescent adoptees. *Journal of American Academy of Child and Adolescent Psychiatry, 34,* 151–159.

# ABOUT THE AUTHORS

Jeanne A. Howard, PhD, Associate Professor of Social Work, and Susan Livingston Smith, MSSW, LCSW, Professor of Social Work, are Codirectors of the Center for Adoption Studies at Illinois State University. They have a longstanding interest in child welfare issues and have published and presented widely on their research related to child welfare adoption. They jointly authored *Promoting Successful Adoptions: Practice with Troubled Families,* as well as many journal articles and monographs on adoption issues. Smith and Howard were honored by the U.S. Department of Health and Human Services with the Adoption Excellence Award in the category of Applied Scholarship and Research in 2000.

# INDEX